Yesterday Today

more of Around Farnham

IN OLD PHOTOGRAPHS

This picture of traffic congestion in Farnham was drawn by Marshall Barnes, a well-known artist in the town. The cartoon was drawn in either 1932 or 1933 and carried the caption: 'The case for road planning'. It shows what was considered to be a typical Saturday morning at the junction of The Borough, West Street and Downing Street. The public house known as The Alliance is now an estate agent's property. When it was a pub, owned by Courage, it was run for a number of years by Jessie Matthews, star of stage, screen and radio, who was known particularly for playing Mrs Dale, of *Mrs Dale's Diary*.

Yesterday Today

more of Around Farnham

IN OLD PHOTOGRAPHS

Collected by JEAN PARRATT

To John,
With many thanks for
your memories and
newspapers.
Jean M Parratt
18-07-05

ALAN SUTTON

Alan Sutton Publishing Limited
Phoenix Mill · Far Thrupp
Stroud · Gloucestershire

First published 1992

For Miriam Vesey-Fitzgerald, a dear friend, who died before this volume was published but who contributed so much to it and for my three colleagues (Ted who married me, Keith who worked with me and Guy who told me to 'Be quiet') to thank them for their tolerance, forbearance and encouragement.

Front cover illustration: These soldiers, showing the 'locals' how to dig trenches, were photographed at Shortfield, Frensham in 1914.

British Library Cataloguing
in Publication Data

Parratt, Jean
Yesterday Today: More of Around Farnham
in Old Photographs
I.Title
942.219

ISBN 0-7509-0114-4

Typeset in 9/10 Sabon.
Typesetting and origination by
Alan Sutton Publishing Limited.
Printed in Great Britain by
The Bath Press, Avon.

Contents

Introduction

People come and shops may go, but the establishment goes on for ever, or so it seems in Farnham.

A visitor to the town in the spring of 1992 who had not seen Farnham for a century would have found that, with very few exceptions (Elphicks, Pullingers and the *Surrey and Hants News* office), it was only the utilities such as the railway station, the fire station, the undertaker and the post office which continue as viable concerns.

The Liberal Club and the Conservative Club remain in the town centre, and the working men's clubs continue to function at Hale, Wrecclesham and Badshot Lea. The centuries-old Farnham Grammar School is now a sixth form college; East Street (later Park) School has closed down and only St Andrew's School, next to the parish church, retains its original name and purpose. Even the large school in West Street, originally intended for boys only, has changed its name and its 'clientele'. Youngsters from five to twelve, both boys and girls, now attend what is called Potter's Gate Church of England Aided First and Middle School.

The visitor from 1892 would, however, still see the twelfth-century castle on the hill, St Andrew's church (the largest parish church in Surrey), the Maltings (now used for arts and recreation, rather than for producing the main ingredient of beer), and the River Wey still flows through the town as it has since time immemorial.

One dramatic change which the 1892 visitor could hardly fail to notice is the concrete monstrosity, as some have called it – The Woolmead – which replaced a row of small shops and houses on the north side of East Street.

Many of the town's public houses were also, a century ago, in East Street, extending from the Royal Deer, on the corner with South Street, eastward towards Aldershot camp. These pubs included the Marlborough Head, the White Hart, the Eagle, the Surrey Arms, the Royal Oak, the Green Man, the Unicorn, the Queen Street Tavern, the Swan and the Seven Stars.

Of these, only the Marlborough Head and the Seven Stars remain as 'watering holes' and the Seven Stars is no longer exactly on the same site as it was when Father Foot, who later moved into a cave in Moor Park, stayed there.

West Street also had its share of pubs and inns, including the Alliance, the

Fox and Hounds, The Wheatsheaf, the Holly Bush, the White Horse, the Fox, the Antelope, the Plough, the Lion and Lamb Tap, the Rainbow and the Black Dragon.

Another trading pattern has changed during the last century. In his book *A Small Boy in the Sixties*, George Sturt recalls aspects of Farnham grocery shops which have long since vanished in the antiseptic world of supermarkets and the vacuum-packed produce of the 1990s. He wrote: 'Sometimes I was sent to a grocer's to get samples of cheese, and these were brought home to try – small cylinders about as big as your little finger – wrapped round in a bit of paper and marked with the price. . . . Sometimes the cheese produced a curious dust which my father used to show us (under a cheap microscope) to be furnished with legs; and sometimes it even yielded little pale maggots.'

Another Farnham author, who was also a skilled photographer and inventor, was John Henry Knight who, in 1909, wrote *Reminiscences of a Country Town (Farnham)*. It is interesting to read Knight's account of the many local turnpikes which existed in his youth and at which travellers had to stop and pay a toll before being able to continue on their journey. He gave details of the turnpikes at Heath End, Bourne Mill, Runfold, Willey (on the Alton Road) and near the Castle. He commented: 'These turnpikes were a great nuisance; I think the usual fee was a penny for a horse, and twopence for a vehicle; this allowed one to return the same day'.

John Henry Knight also gave his opinion about the names of several fields at Badshot Lea, including Gallows Field, which he suggests was where Royalists were hanged during the Civil War. Others possibly with a similar origin to their names are Scraggeries, Hoarse Crokers and Bloody Bones. According to the Oxford Dictionary, the verb to scrag means to hang on a gallows or to wring the neck. It sounds as if Badshot Lea had more than its fair share of places of execution.

Some surnames are particularly common in the Farnham area, including Fry, Pharo, Parratt and Pullinger. Hale is an area where many people are named Pharo. Most of the family's members were brickmakers in the past, probably working at the Old Park Brickworks. John Henry Knight, ever adventurous in his theories, suggested that this name came from the Pharaoh, King of Egypt, who compelled the Israelites to make bricks.

Farnham's first workhouse was built in 1726, almost opposite the parish church, and was replaced in 1790 by one in the Hale Road. One person whose death there is well documented is William Foot, the man who first appeared in Farnham in October 1839, when he stayed at the Seven Stars in East Street. One morning a certain William Tilbury, who was described in the 1841 census as being 'a 70-year-old post boy', was engaged by Foot to load a wheelbarrow with a portmanteau, a cloak, a carpet bag, luggage and a hat, and push it to Moor Park from the Seven Stars.

On 14 January 1840 Samuel White, a labourer, saw a man lying wet and cold on the path near Mother Ludlam's cave in Moor Park. The man, who it emerged was Foot, was taken first to a cottage and later to the workhouse, where he died the same day.

Foot had tried to live in Mother Ludlam's cave, but it was too wet, so he excavated another, higher up the bank, which could only be entered by a man on his hands and knees. The owner of Moor Park saw a way to exploit this unfortunate event, and for some time he charged twopence (a considerable sum at the time) for sightseers to view Foot's cave.

As a small child Nellie Foot (now named Stephens, and believed to be a distant relative of William Foot) lived in Bridge Square, while her father, Ern, worked at Farnham Maltings. In a short story about the Maltings, called *Beyond the Black Gates*, she writes: 'The first thing I noticed was the pleasant smell of the barley and malt. The malt came tumbling out of a long chute, which came from another part of the building upstairs, into a sack. When this was full it was stood aside and another sack was put into position to be filled. The full sacks were tied and stood with others to be taken to the brewery (Courage and Co.) in Alton.

'Occasionally if dad had time he would show me over the whole building, explaining what everything was for. I saw the barley in soak. It lay in long troughs filled with water for about two days and nights. I watched the men spreading the washed barley across the floor. It made me think of a well-kept allotment garden, the edges being very tidy and straight, the barley being about four feet deep.

'It would be turned over at intervals. The drying rooms were above the furnaces. They had floors composed of tiles with tiny holes.'

Farnham has been well known for its clay for centuries, with potteries in the area since Roman times. Six hundred years ago it was also famous for the huge oak trees which grew around the town. Anyone visting Westminster Hall, in London, will see what has been described as both the greatest achievement in the history of woodworking and as the eighth wonder of the world. The subject of this acclaim is the hammer-beam roof, which was constructed in Farnham from enormous oaks, under the leadership of Hugh Herland. In 1395 it was moved by wain, wagon and barge, to Westminster. It then took five years to set the huge trusses in position and complete the roof, covering a building which was 239 ft long by 69 ft wide. In spite of its area, the roof was constructed in such a way that there are no supporting pillars for the whole of its length.

The exact spot in Farnham where this roof was made has never been identified, though Hugh Herland, the creator of this staggering feat, who worked without the benefit of modern cranes, is still regarded as Britain's greatest carpenter.

So what links these diverse events and talents? Farnham, from animal skin-clad Mesolithic men of yesterday to fashionably-clad women of today, this town has been, and still is home.

SECTION ONE

People at Large

People are the most interesting thing in life. No two are exactly the same in their looks or thoughts, and each one is different in his or her outlook on life and the world in general. Different occupations necessitate the acquisition of different skills, whether learning how to gauge the value of junk or how to correctly diagnose appendicitis. In the following pages are some of the people who have made their mark in both small and large ways in Farnham over the past century.

Farnham has had many amateur, but extremely capable, photographers, from John Henry Knight, of early motor car fame, to those of the present day. One of the younger men to capture the town on film is Jonathan Durham, who snapped Charlie Wenham, the rag and bone merchant, while he and his faithful horse were resting on the grass at the end of Farnham bypass.

Mr Littlejohn taking rolls from the oven at Worsam's Bakery in Downing Street. This bakery operated for 200 years under the same name until it closed in the 1980s. The two cottage loaves which were carved on the fascia board of the shop can still be seen on that of the newsagent, now on the former baker's site.

Percival Pelling as a telegraph boy at Frensham in 1913. Perce and his wife, Rosie, celebrated their Diamond Wedding anniversary in February 1992 and were featured on the back of the *Surrey and Hants News* because they had kept that newspaper's cutting, describing their wedding, for sixty years.

Before the River Wey was widened this was a familiar sight in Farnham, every time the river overflowed. The water level rose halfway up Downing Street, and even today the signs of former flooding can still be seen in the street. This is a view along the bottom of Downing Street, looking towards Gostrey Meadow.

The Bessant sisters who ran a laundry at Holt Pound, across the cricket ground from what was once the Forest Inn (now the Merrie Monks). The ladies were said to be particularly tiny but when they died and their laundry fell into ruin, I saw the remainder of their equipment – a mangle, old baths and many dolly pegs. If they were as short as legend tells they must have found turning the mangle and stretching up to the lines very tiring indeed.

Harold Falkner, one of Farnham's best known architects, was also considered by some to be an eccentric. This characteristic paid off because he bought tiles, bricks, and shop fronts, including that on the present day *Surrey and Hants News* office at No. 104a West Street, which might otherwise have been destroyed. Though a road is named after Mr Falkner, it is for the design of the buildings he created, many of them at Dippenhall and Crondall, that the man will be remembered. Falkner is seen here wearing the famous hat which was once used to extinguish a fire in a motor car.

Raymond Foster, cobbler and shoemaker, who operated from a small shop in Downing Street, still run by his son today. He once made a pair of boots for a paratrooper to wear as he walked across America and, upon the paratrooper's return, the shoes were on display in his shop window.

aily Mirror

YOUR MINIATURE FOR NOTHING. (See page 6.)

MONDAY, NOVEMBER 14, 1904. One Halfpenny.

BISHOP OF WINCHESTER KICKS OFF AT A FOOTBALL GAME.

Dr. Ryle started the game between Farnham and Haslemere, an event in the Surrey Junior Cup, at Farnham on Saturday. The first photograph shows the Bishop leaving his seat to kick. The second shows the actual kick.

It is not every day that a cleric starts a football match, which is probably the reason that the *Daily Mirror* chose to feature the Bishop of Winchester, who lived at Farnham Castle, on its front page of 14 November 1904. A street on a housing estate in Farnham is named after the bishop, Dr Ryle.

Olave, Lady Baden Powell, wife of the founder of the Boy Scount and Girl Guide movements was courted by her husband after a most unusual meeting. It was said that he, Robert, had first seen his future wife when one was going up an escalator and the other was travelling down. He was so enamoured of her that he covered the same route, day after day, until he saw her again as, in the words of an old song, 'I saw her once as she came passing by but yet I love her 'til I die'. For several years they lived at Pax Hill, Bentley, a few miles out of Farnham.

Spider the dog, whose master was Farnham postman S.J. Hall, was also not averse to a bit of letter carrying. Pictured here in Upper Church Lane in the town centre in the 1920s, are Mr Hall's daughters, Lily and May, with Spider, who was once used to carry a message tied to his collar into the hop gardens, possibly those which then existed off Crondall Lane.

The family firm of John Goodridge in Downing Street, made some overalls specially for the largest man in Farnham in 1958. He was 'Tiny' Sawkins, who lived in Guildford Road. Before Mr Sawkins took possession of them, however, two of the shop assistants, Wally Dudley, right, and Doug Saunders, wore them at the same time, each having his own two legs down one leg of the dungarees. Wally married a lady called Peggy Ward. A shop selling fabrics and haberdashery, called Ward's, was situated opposite to Goodridge's for many years.

A.J. Stevens, solicitor, in his garden in Ford Lane, wearing a large-brimmed straw hat. He was a renowned storyteller, at least to his children, and would make up mysteries to amuse them. Lancelot, John, Michael and Miriam, his offspring, appear in many places on the pages of this book.

Four large murals are now on the walls of Farnham Library, on loan from Farnham Museum. They show workers in the Crosby factory during the Second World War and they were painted by John Hutton, the internationally famous glass engraver. In this picture are two of the female workers who appeared in the murals, Winnie Webster and Joan Wright. Other women who worked in the factory and who were captured on canvas by John Hutton were Rose Turner, Dot Birks and Dot Gilliam.

Walter Aspden, a police constable with the Surrey Constabulary, became a traffic warden after he retired. Before that time, however, he had been a boxer in the police team, and in 1950 he won the European Police Championship at the Albert Hall. A man named Sullivan, whose brother had been Middleweight Champion of England, asked Walter if he would like a few rounds with Alex Buxton. Mr Aspden said he thought he would because it would give him some kudos for coming events. That was about 1951. He was also adept at cross-country running and tug-of-war, although he was once stopped from boxing because his superintendent said it interfered with his police work. Later he was allowed to continue. In the top picture Wally, right, is shaking Alex Buxton's hand. Below he can be seen booking a motorist in West Street, Farnham.

Sir John Verney, one of the town's most hard-working councillors. He was one of the first to see the value of saving Farnham Maltings for the town, and he also formed the Nowhere club in East Street for youngsters when there was no youth club. He is an author and artist, and from the 1950s to the 1970s was a household name in the town.

Bernard Nicholas Nathanial Woodward MC was vicar of Hale from 1923 to 1928. He had been a cleric in South Africa, but decided to return to England and took a living at Hale. Unfortunately his wife died and, finding himself alone, the vicar decided to return once more to South Africa.

The gentleman in the centre of this group, photographed in a garden in West Street, is believed to be Will Jackman, often described as 'the smartest man in Farnham'. His tailoring business was in West Street, close to The Wheatsheaf, and he would often leave his counter and nip into the pub for 'a quick half'. He always drank halves rather than pints but he drank a lot of the smaller measures. One of his tall stories, after a number of halves, was his claim that it was his grandfather who had pushed the Isle of Wight away from the mainland of England.

Dr G.H. Roberts, for many years one of Farnham's most respected and best-loved doctors.

Richard Dufty, who was for many years Master of the Armouries at the Tower of London. He was also Secretary to the Royal Commission on Historical Monuments and later Vice-Chairman of the Cathedrals Advisory Committee. Locally he was Chairman of the Governors of Farnham Art School from 1953 to 1964 and President of the Farnham Museum Society. He moved from Farnham in the spring of 1992.

David Lloyd George, politican and prime minister, who lived at Churt, near Farnham, for many years with his mistress, Frances. After his wife died he married Frances, who had been his secretary. The Pride of the Valley public house at Churt has a sign on which his portrait is painted.

Four judges at what was probably Rowledge Flower Show. In the 1950s and 1960s flower shows and allotment exhibitions were considered a major part of the local scene, and members of the Women's Institute and other local bodies would judge the work and growing powers of their fellow townspeople. Second from left in this picture is Madge Green, a journalist and author, who is also renowned for her flower arranging prowess. Her husband was both editor of the *Surrey and Hants News* and later of the *Aldershot News*. To the left of Mrs Green is Mrs Hyde, whose husband, Ted, was well known as the man in charge of the town's water rate collection.

A family Christmas in 1925. Florence Julius, later Stevens, was born in 1846. Nearly a century of Farnham history was recorded by this lady in her simple exercise books, and a resumé of them was published in the Farnham and District Museum Society Newsletter in March 1988. Her daughter-in-law, Mary, is in the second row, second from left. Her grandchildren, John, Miriam, Lancelot and Michael each had the name of Julius as one of their first names. In her book To *The Vicarage Born: Memoirs of Florence Julius 1846–1937*, Miriam Vesey-Fitzgerald describes the life of Florence, who married into the Stevens family. It includes a considerable amount about local churches and clergy. Her father was the Rev Henry Richards Julius, who arrived in Farnham in 1839 for his first and only curacy. He had been ordained by Bishop Sumner (who founded both Hale Schools and St John's church at Hale) and is buried in the churchyard there. Florence recalled that her father was the curate for Hale and that every day for the first year of his curacy he walked across Farnham Park to visit the squatters or gypsies, a wild and lawless lot (although there were a few exceptions), who lived there. It was Mr Julius' lot to raise funds for the building of St John's church, and perhaps it was he who decided that hogs' heads should be at the top of each pillar in the aisle.

SECTION TWO

Enterprise Zone

Whatever work one undertakes, whether for oneself or for a company, there is always a degree of enterprise needed to make the job seem worthwhile. In this section the enterprise factor runs from the man growing plants in his back garden, to sell to the public, through to the men who met with disgust the news that their brickworks was to close. Nevertheless, stoical as only the British workman can be, they met the challenge head on and found other work to keep their families in food and clothes.

Ted Cane, sitting in The Borough, at the side of W.H. Smith, selling the flowers and other plants which he grew in his garden in West Street. As a boy he lived in Red Lion Lane, and was a close neighbour of Nellie Stephens, who is quoted in the introduction.

Dzus Fasteners Factory on the Farnham Trading Estate, soon after it was built in 1952. Forty years on the building is now to be demolished to make way for a Sainsbury's superstore.

Gas ceased to be produced in Farnham in 1953, but it was a few more years before the famous landmark of the Retort House, in East Street, was demolished.

This row of shops was demolished to make way for the current branch of Sainsbury's in South Street. The shops seen on p. 68 had already been demolished (a row of notices pasted up on the wall of a remaining shop show where) and soon Cullen's the grocery shop, Pococks the baker (centre), the Oxfam shop, Farnham's first charity shop, and Look In, another charity shop run by Farnham Lions, were all razed to the ground in the name of progress.

The men in this picture have just heard that their place of employment, known as the Old Park Brickworks, is to close in a few weeks' time. The owner of the firm was the Sussex & Dorking United Brick Company in Horsham. Back row, left to right: H. Stokes, H. Rickwood. Front row: W. Chapple, L. Strudwick, R. Stokes, A.D. Watmore (foreman), H. Lewington, P. Court, W. Lodge.

The ground floor of Elphicks in 1957. The blouse on the stand in the centre is priced at 47/6d and the two-piece costume on the left bears a label carrying the price of £5 19s 6d.

The Farnham Music Warehouse was situated in South Street, but it is not known exactly where. As James Brewer was said to be the 'local secretary for Victoria College of Music', one must assume that he was relatively well known. Mr Brewer, the advertisement states, also made 'Periodical Visits to Headley, Hindhead and District for Tuning and Repairs'.

SECTION THREE

Taking a Breather

Although there were few opportunities in the past for working people to take a breather during their hours of toil, the presence of a photographer ensured that work stopped, at least for a few minutes. Later, as tea breaks became law, there were more opportunities to have a rest while at work, even though some breaks, such as that experienced by the bus driver in one of the pictures in this section, may have been more frustrating than relaxing.

The lady in the centre of this picture is obviously having an easier time than the woman, extreme right, who is still sitting picking her hops off the bine in spite of the fact that a photographer was at the scene. In spite of his adult clothes the boy, second from the left, is very young, perhaps not more than fourteen, but he was doing a man's work in one of Farnham's hop gardens in the 1920s.

Maurice Birch, whose home was in Roman Way, had this picture taken for inclusion in the *Surrey and Hants News* in May 1960. He was a groundsman for Farnham Urban District Council and was snapped next to a Davidia tree in Gostrey Meadow. The tree, more commonly known as the pocket handkerchief tree, is also sometimes called the dove tree or ghost tree because of the appearance of the leaves. While Mr Birch worked on the grounds he always kept a watchful eye on the children, and at least twice rescued youngsters in difficulty – a three-year-old in the water whose mother was shouting 'Save my baby', and an invalid child who was strapped in a heavy wheelchair which had rolled into the river.

William Newell, left, and his brother Frank can be seen at Badshot Farm around 1910, while William was working there for Humphrey Gardener, the farm's tenant. The farm owner was John Henry Knight. When Mr Gardener moved to Mavins Road, William went with him as his gardener.

When Farnham Post Office was being rebuilt in West Street, the staff operated from a unit in Bear Lane for almost four years. This inside view of the temporary sorting office in 1970 shows Doug Tanner, left (postmaster), and Mick Taylor, taking a break from their labours.

This elderly lady, standing at the door of one of the almshouses in Castle Street, was possibly waiting for a postman to arrive. She was Miss Fanny Foot, a relative of Mr Foot who once ran a number of pubs in the town. The photograph was taken in 1946.

Irene Brown helped her father, Arthur, clean windows throughout the Second World War, while her brother, also Arthur, was away on armed services. This picture was taken in South Street close to its junction with East Street.

Arthur Brown, senior, followed in his father's footsteps and started pushing a window-cleaning cart around Farnham when he left school. In this picture Arthur, who can also be seen in the photograph above, takes a breather before starting his afternoon round from Buller's Road, Weybourne. Today a third generation of 'Mr Brown the Window Cleaner', now in his late fifties, still cleans the town's shop windows.

Miriam Stevens, later the wife of writer, author and broadcaster Brian Vesey-Fitzgerald, dressed in costume for the 1930 Farnham Pageant. She is accompanied by her father, Alfred. Miriam was nineteen when this picture was taken. The first Farnham Pageant was held in 1910 to raise £800 – the money still owed on the building of Church House in Union Road. It was repeated in 1930 and again in 1950, being held each time in the grounds of Farnham Castle. In the late 1980s it was performed once more but in a new format. Several people who had been in the 1910 production appeared again in 1930. At least one man, Harold Cole (see p. 90), took part in 1930, 1950 and 1988.

The grocery firm of William Kingham, in West Street built a warehouse in The Hart in 1953. A time capsule was embedded in the brickwork at the entrance to the building, and this can be seen marked by a concrete plaque. When the building was demolished in the mid-1980s, to make way for a supermarket and car park, some of the original items in the time capsule were placed in the wall of the Lion and Lamb Courtyard development. The houses in the far background of the picture are at the top of Crondall Lane.

Crosbys, which was once Farnham's biggest employer, assembled its staff outside one of its units, either in East Street or South Street, for a photo call in 1918. Only five women are in the picture but the row of young boys at the front, some wearing caps, shows that about a quarter of the workforce at that time were children.

The *Farnham Herald*, which celebrates its centenary in 1992, was founded by E.W. Langham. A thousand copies were produced of the first issue, from a printing works in South Street, similar to that on p. 52. Mr Langham was twenty-one and had been in the trade for only three years. He cycled to Farnham to see the printing works, which had been advertised in *The Printer's Register*. It had been owned by Mr Frampton Ames. In this picture Frank Burningham, left, discusses with Mr Langham a later version of the *Farnham Herald*, when it became a broadsheet.

During the 1960s this young woman worked for the *Farnham Herald*'s rival newspaper, the *Surrey and Hants News* (see p. 51). Her name was Janice Spedding and the freelance photographer who took this shot, Edward Griffith, described her as 'the most attractive girl I've ever captured on film'. She was standing on a bridge over the River Wey in Borelli Gardens. Now Janice Cowan, she has three grown-up children, lives in Canada, writes children's books and is still a journalist.

The present Farnham police station was in the process of being constructed when this picture was taken, in the mid-1960s. On the left is Owen Hall, above the local branch of the Co-operative Society, and Gostrey Meadow is on the right. Traffic was still two-way in Union Road. The grocery department of the Co-op had recently become self-service, and the pulley system in the ceiling for taking cash straight to the office by means of a wire and small pots, had been removed. Dances were held in Owen Hall. Heath and Wiltshire owned a garage which can be noted by the Mobil sign far right (see p. 141).

Known as The White Post Stores, the small shop at the junction of Adam's Park Road and Hale Road was for many years run by Leonard Hale, left, and his son Robert, right. Today the shop is a private house. There seems to have been a cleaning campaign in progress when this picture was taken, because almost every item in the window is Lux soap flakes or Wisk, a detergent popular in 1952 when the picture was taken.

Photographed by Wendy Hobart in the 1940s, this scene at the junction of Bear Lane, The Borough, East Street and South Street, is typical of the time when only a couple of cars a minute went through the crossroads and Farnham was a sleepy, country market town.

Inside the Crosby factory in 1918. The workshop was heated by a large black iron stove (foreground). The women are wearing long white overalls over their normal clothing. Crosby Doors, the name which the company adopted after the Second World War, closed its Farnham branch in 1991.

Another picture inside Crosby's in 1918. The very young workers are wearing their caps, even inside the building, and there does not seem to be a guard on any of the pieces of machinery or belt-driven lathes.

This group of six men, including Andrew Crosby, dressed in high collars, waistcoats, ties and in one case, gaiters, pose outside the factory in 1918. Within a few minutes they were back inside with all the cares and worries that senior positions in firms hold. The Crosby story began in 1877, the year in which the first public telephone call was made. When Andrew Crosby opened the firm at No. 97 East Street, he operated as a plumber, painter, glazier, gas-fitter and paper-hanger. By 1903, when the firm became known as Crosby & Co., it was also listed as a monumental mason and a builder.

The workforce at the *Farnham Herald* when Ernest Langham first started up the presses. The owner is on the left, wearing a bow tie, with some of his printers, each of whom set separate letters into rods to make the lines of type used in the newspaper (see p. 52).

The Runfold Roadshop, owned by Jim Tice of Badshot Lea, toured the surrounding villages in the 1950s and 1960s. This scene appears to show two women who are talking about the purchases made by the one on the right before the other one climbs on to the van to buy her 'country-baked bread, groceries and confectionery'. The roadshop was part of the Runfold Bakery operation.

Badshot Lea Docks have been famous locally for most of this century, ever since the first *Saucy Kipper* was built by the River Blackwater (little more than a stream) for a carnival in 1904. In July 1959, the *Saucy Kipper III* was snapped outside the village school before the carnival began, and the bus driver could do nothing but sit and wait for the frivolities to end. The 'ship' was built by Charles Backhurst and Sam Hewins and won first prize. Riding in the bows are Cheryl and Sharon Smith. Two of the oldest, and lifelong residents of the village, Mrs Cope and Mr Patrick, are on the bridge and Sea Rangers stood smartly to attention aft. The skirts worn by the young ladies on the right were held out by layers of net – the fashionable style of petticoat for teenagers at that time.

Leighton's Optical Workshop employees in 1959, outside the company's works in Bear Lane. Back row, left to right: ? Pink, ? Spencer, ? Willgoss, ? Collett, ? Mills, ? Clark. Middle row: ? Barr, ? Elford, ? Rose, ? Youldon, ? Ellis, ? Cannon, ? Rayer, ? Roffey, ? Lenfestey, ? Richardson, ? Martin. Front: ? Zepke, ? Elford.

In complete contrast to the high-powered businessman is this picture of youth and old age together in the garden of Little Twynax, Ford Lane. George Nixon was the gardener who also cleaned the boots and shoes of the Stevens family (see p. 106), but early in the 1920s Mr Nixon sat down for a few minutes in the sunshine with young Michael Stevens, who is sockless and has his tunic held at the waist by a belt.

SECTION FOUR

Ephemera

Printed or handwritten items which are intended for use for a short time only and are then thrown away are known as ephemera. Newspapers, theatre programmes and bus tickets all come into this heading, as do explanatory leaflets, menus and price lists. Some people keep such items for sentimental reasons, while others only come to light when floorboards are lifted or fireplaces removed. Some such pieces are included in this section.

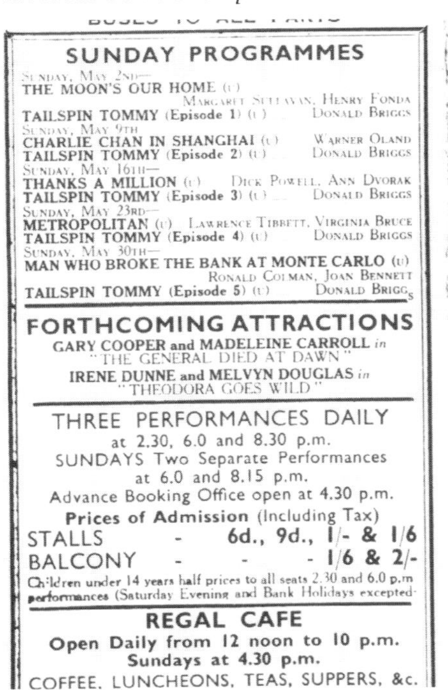

SUNDAY PROGRAMMES

SUNDAY, MAY 2ND—
THE MOON'S OUR HOME (U) MARGARET SULLAVAN, HENRY FONDA
TAILSPIN TOMMY (Episode 1) (U) DONALD BRIGGS
SUNDAY, MAY 9TH
CHARLIE CHAN IN SHANGHAI (U) WARNER OLAND
TAILSPIN TOMMY (Episode 2) (U) DONALD BRIGGS
SUNDAY, MAY 16TH—
THANKS A MILLION (U) DICK POWELL, ANN DVORAK
TAILSPIN TOMMY (Episode 3) (U) DONALD BRIGGS
SUNDAY, MAY 23RD—
METROPOLITAN (U) LAWRENCE TIBBETT, VIRGINIA BRUCE
TAILSPIN TOMMY (Episode 4) (U) DONALD BRIGGS
SUNDAY, MAY 30TH—
MAN WHO BROKE THE BANK AT MONTE CARLO (U) RONALD COLMAN, JOAN BENNETT
TAILSPIN TOMMY (Episode 5) (U) DONALD BRIGGS

FORTHCOMING ATTRACTIONS

GARY COOPER and MADELEINE CARROLL in "THE GENERAL DIED AT DAWN"
IRENE DUNNE and MELVYN DOUGLAS in "THEODORA GOES WILD"

THREE PERFORMANCES DAILY
at 2.30, 6.0 and 8.30 p.m.
SUNDAYS Two Separate Performances at 6.0 and 8.15 p.m.
Advance Booking Office open at 4.30 p.m.
Prices of Admission (Including Tax)
STALLS - 6d., 9d., 1/- & 1/6
BALCONY - - - 1/6 & 2/-
Children under 14 years half prices to all seats 2.30 and 6.0 p.m performances (Saturday Evening and Bank Holidays excepted)

REGAL CAFE
Open Daily from 12 noon to 10 p.m.
Sundays at 4.30 p.m.
COFFEE, LUNCHEONS, TEAS, SUPPERS, &c.

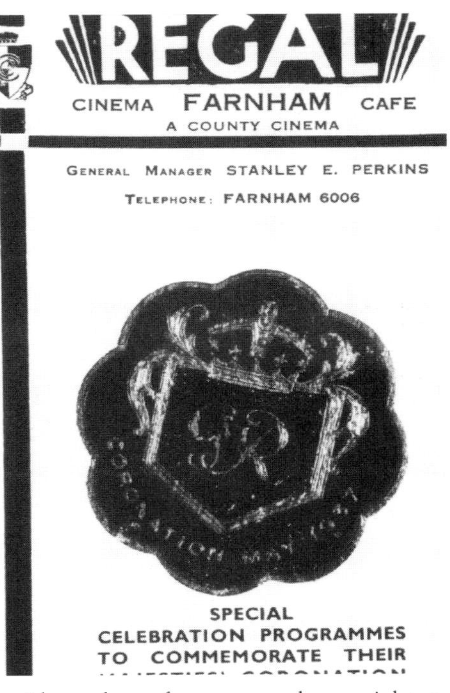

REGAL
CINEMA FARNHAM CAFE
A COUNTY CINEMA
GENERAL MANAGER STANLEY E. PERKINS
TELEPHONE: FARNHAM 6006
SPECIAL CELEBRATION PROGRAMMES TO COMMEMORATE THEIR

The Regal Cinema opened in Farnham in 1933 with a gala performance and a special programme in mottled green and 'spider's web' transparent paper between each sheet. Mr Stanley Perkins was the manager then, as he was at the time of the coronation in 1937 when, as this picture shows, there was a special celebration programme to commemorate the event. Coffee, luncheons, teas and suppers could all be enjoyed in the café on the first floor. A back seat in the stalls cost 1s 6d and the full programme was shown three times a day during the week and twice on Sundays.

VOL. XI. No. 7. PRICE ONE PENNY. JULY, 1907.

Farnham Congregational Church Magazine.

SERVICES.

SUNDAY—

PUBLIC WORSHIP
11 a.m. and 6.30 p.m.

SUNDAY SCHOOL (East Street) 9.45 a.m. and 2 30 p.m.

The Lord's Supper first Sunday in each month.

MONDAY—

MOTHERS' MEETING
2 p.m.

*MUTUAL IMPROVEMENT SOCIETY 8 p.m.

*BAND OF HOPE 7 p.m.

*Alternate weeks.

Photograph by Valentine and Sons, Dundee.

SERVICES.

THURSDAY—

WEEK-NIGHT SERVICE
7.30 p m.

Y. P. S. C. E. 8.20 .m

FRIDAY—

JUNIOR Y. P. S. C. E.
7 p.m.

CHOIR PRACTICE
8.30 p.m.

Minister—REV. T. W. INGRAM.

Assistant Minister—Rev. D. DARLOW, Bourne, Shortfield and Wrecclesham.

Church Secretary—Mr. A. H. BARLING.
Church Treasurer – Mr. A. J. BENTALL.

Printed at the "Surrey and Hants News" Office, 1, Borough, Farnham

In 1907 the *Farnham Congregational Church* (now the United Reformed Church) *Magazine* had its cover printed locally and with information pertinent to its congregation. This piece of ephemera came to light when a shop in The Borough was gutted in 1978. The magazine was printed by the *Surrey and Hants News* when it was still sited at No. 1 The Borough. The Church Secretary was Mr A.H. Barling and the treasurer was Mr A.J. Bentall.

DIOCESE OF WINCHESTER

This is to Certify that Lottie Nash
has passed a specially satisfactory
Examination in Religious Knowledge
in the Frensham School
on the undermentioned dates :-
Feb 18th 1897

Diocesan Inspector.
Rector.
Bishop of the Diocese.

Although at first sight there seems nothing to connect these two items, they are joined by religion. Young Lottie Nash received the certificate on the right for her examination in religious knowledge at Frensham School, on 18 February 1897. Almost ninety years later, during Farnham Fortnight, the town was chosen as a venue for BBC television's *Songs of Praise*. During the run-up to the programme views of Farnham were shown, taken from a vantage point above Farnham Maltings. One of these showed the nineteenth-century horse-drawn bus for which this ticket was bought. The programme was filmed in a summer heatwave and shown in the winter. Controversy surrounded the programme when a man bared his bottom on the bus and was seen to do so on television.

F.G.G.S.

Farnham Girls' Grammar School and
Old Girls' Association
March, 1953

THE
FARNHAMIAN

VOL. 40 No. 1 JULY, 1953

Boys benefited from grammar school education in Farnham for hundreds of years before the girls were considered. The boys were first educated in a room in the parish church, later moved to West Street and in 1906 went to the purpose-built premises in Morley Road. Soon after they started lessons here the first of *The Farnhamian* magazines was published and from then until the amalgamation of the two schools in the 1970s, it faithfully recorded results of football matches, Boy Scout meetings, boxing bouts and shooting, among other things. Details were also included about old boys, including deaths and marriages. In this issue mention is made of a happy event: 'Congratulations to A. Barter on the birth of a daughter in February.' No information is given about the mother of this baby girl. The FGGS magazine shows the girls' school built in the 1930s, less than half a mile from the boys' unit, but there was little contact (officially) between the pupils.

The Shop at 10/11 West Street, Farnham, from 1960

...epared from information by Mr. F. W. Simmonds, Mr. George Smith of Tongham, and others.

10, West Street, FARNHAM, Surrey . . . . . . in 18

Here was born the author of a Famous Hyn

Rock of ages, cleft for me.
Let me hide myself in Thee:
Let the Water and the Blood,
From Thy riven Side which flow'd,
Be of sin the double cure,
Cleanse me from its guilt and power.

Not the labours of my hands
Can fulfil Thy law's demands:
Could my zeal no respite know,

Nothing in my hand I bring,
Simply to Thy Cross I cling;
Naked, come to Thee for dress;
Helpless, look to Thee for grace;
Foul, I to the Fountain fly;
Wash me, Saviour, or I die.

While I draw this fleeting breath,
When my eyelids close in death,
When I soar to tracts unknown,

Augustus Montague Toplady was born in West Street, Farnham in 1740. Today a piece of stone taken from Burrington Coombe in Somerset records the birth of the man who has become world famous for his hymn *Rock of ages, cleft for me*. The picture on the right shows the lodging house as it was when Major Richard Toplady and his wife, in town on a visit, were unable to find accommodation at an inn and had to stay in what was then a small house. A fireplace recently found in the cellar of the building on the right (which replaced the one in the left hand picture in 1875) is believed to have been in the kitchen of the building when Toplady was born. Elphicks, who own the building, extensively renovated it again in 1991–2. The stone giving details of Toplady can be seen between the third and fourth windows on the first floor in the left hand picture.

Sir, Sept. 29th 1817

The Favor of your Company is desired at the Goat's Head on Wednesday, ~~the~~ 1st of Oct.

Dinner at half-past 1 o'Clock

This visiting card, although faded, survived behind a fireplace in Downing Street for 168 years before being found. One wonders if the appointment at the Goat's Head (in The Borough facing the bottom of Castle Street) was kept on Wednesday 1 October 1817.

COALS AT FARNHAM STATION.

W. & J. MASON'S

Present Prices

FOR CASH.

	PER TON
WALLSEND (Seaborne)	23s.
DERBYSHIRE COAL (nearly equal to Seaborne, and free from dust)........	21s.
MIDLAND COAL (a large and useful article for cottagers & ordinary purposes	19s.
HARTLEY'S and other Brickburners, Bakers, and Steam Coal	17s. to 21s.
TANFIELD'S for Blacksmiths	20s.
ANTHRACITE for malting, hop-drying, &c.	30s.
COKE, Best Gas, for ironing-stoves, &c....	26s.
,, For Ironfounders..................	32s.

BY THE TRUCK LOAD, 6d. PER TON LESS, AND A FURTHER REDUCTION IN A QUANTITY.

Carting 1s. per ton into the town, and 9d. per ton per mile, to any part of the country adjacent.

Found at the same time as the visiting card above was this card listing the prices of coal from W. & J. Mason at Farnham Station. There were once more than twenty coal merchants in town but now only one, Comley's, remains. In May 1857 Derbyshire coal, described as being free from dust, cost 21s per ton. Carting from the station into the town centre cost 1s per ton and 9d per mile to any part of the 'country adjacent'. These prices applied only to cash customers.

Just out of town at Gong Hill was a hotel known as Morris Lodge. The twelve page brochure gives details of 'bus services which passed the door four times an hour, taking eight minutes to reach Farnham Station. From there an electric train would take one hour to reach London. Terms, all inclusive, were 5 gns per week or 17s 6d per day, with bed and breakfast costing 10s 6d. The proprietor when this brochure was printed was Frank L. Vincent-Jones.

For centuries the Lion and Lamb courtyard has been a place to which visitors to the town went for accommodation or to drink in the hostelry which was once on the site. Today a coffee shop occupies part of the building which housed a café which had this as a tariff card. A lion and lamb can be seen as the logo. On the reverse are details of charges – a Cornish tea (tea, scones, jam, cream and cakes) cost 1s 4d and a pot of China tea was 6d per person.

LION & LAMB
CAFE
FARNHAM

Phone : Farnham 434

Tariff

Saturday, May 30th	CONCERT BY CHILDREN'S CHOIR FIREWORK DISPLAY COMMUNITY SINGING	Church House Farnham Park
Sunday, May 31st	PARADE OF ORGANISATIONS TO CIVIC SERVICE	Farnham Parish Church
Monday, June 1st	CONCERT BY BOYD NEEL ORCHESTRA OLD TIME BALL	Girls' Grammar School Memorial Hall
Tuesday, June 2nd	PEALING OF BELLS CONCERT OF MILITARY MUSIC (Aldershot Band) CROWNING OF CARNIVAL QUEEN DANCING :: FIREWORKS	Gostrey Meadow
Wednesday, June 3rd	GRAND CARNIVAL PROCESSION Presentation of Prizes MOTOR CYCLE GYMKHANA	Gostrey Meadow Farnham Park
Thursday, June 4th	VARIOUS DISPLAYS Musical Interludes — Farnham Youth Orchestra	Gostrey Meadow
Friday, June 5th	For older folks aged 70 years and over TEA AND ENTERTAINMENT By JANE WORTH (London) and LOCAL ARTISTES. Tickets: W.V.S. GRAND CORONATION BALL	Gostrey Meadow Memorial Hall
Saturday, June 6th	SPORTS DAY POPULAR DANCE MADRIGALS	Memorial Ground and Hall Old Vicarage
Sunday, June 7th	DISPLAY BY ST. JOHN AMBULANCE BRIGADE SPECIAL FESTIVAL CHOIR—Coronation Music	Memorial Ground Farnham Parish Church
All Week	EXHIBITION OF PAINTINGS AND VISUAL ART LOCAL SHOPS: WINDOW DISPLAY—COMPETITIONS	School of Art See Brochure
Thursday, June 11th 6 Days	Farnham Amateur Operatic Society present "MERRIE ENGLAND"	Gostrey Meadow

1Jv2827

ALDERSHOT & DISTRICT TRACTION COMPANY, LTD

SINGLE

The number of the stage at which the passenger enters the omnibus must be printed on the ticket and the passenger is entitled to travel to the stage point corresponding to the value of the fare paid as shewn on fare table. This ticket must be shewn or given up on demand and is issued subject to the regulations as printed in the Company's Time Tables.

DATE | JOURNEY NO. | STAGE BOARDED | SHILLINGS | PENCE

Bell Punch Company, London.

When Queen Elizabeth II was crowned in 1953, Farnham went to town on its celebrations. Morris and Sons, printers from Lower Bourne, were asked to produce a special programme of events and duly came up with 'the works'. The celebrations lasted from 30 May to 17 June. Gostrey Meadow, Farnham Park, the School of Art in West Street (formerly the Farnham Grammar School), the Memorial Hall and ground, Church House, the parish church and the Girls' Grammar School were all venues for events during the celebration fortnight.

The whole of the Farnham area was once served by the Yellow Bus company and the Aldershot and District Traction Company, affectionately known as 'Have a shot and risk it'. Whenever someone took a journey on an ADTCO bus or coach, the ticket, such as that on the left, was the receipt. The thin card ticket was printed with sequence numbers, quite unlike the thin, paper receipts which are issued in the 1990s for bus journeys.

Surrey and  Hants News,

FARNHAM ADVERTISER, GUILDFORD TIMES, ALDERSHOT GAZETTE.

No. 1147.—NEW SERIES. FARNHAM : SATURDAY, APRIL 9, 1881. ONE PENNY.

Births, Marriages, and Deaths.

In Memoriam.

Money advanced.

Money Lent without Publicity.

Bragg's Vegetable Charcoal

Sinclair's Cold Water Soap

ARTHUR DASHWOOD & Co.,
Horticultural Engineers,
THE SYCAMORE WORKS, EAST STREET, FARNHAM.

Don't Miss This Opportunity.
GREAT SALE
DRAPERY, CARPETS, HATS, MANTLES, ETC., ETC.
MESSRS. J. J. HAZELL & Co.
SURPLUS WINTER STOCK,
2s. 6d. IN THE £.
Don't forget—2s. 6d. in the Pound.

CHARLES KERN,
EAST STREET, FARNHAM.
Carriages of every description built on the premises.
Carriages Repaired and Painted. Estimates Given.
New and second-hand dog carts and whitechapel carts.

NOTICE.

M. & J. TILY,
Furnishing and General Ironmongers,
7, Castle Street, and Long Garden Works,
FARNHAM.

LAWN MOWERS.
The "AUTOMATON"
The "REVERSIBLE"
The "GLOBE"
The "HORSE POWER"
The "COVENTRY" and other MOWERS.
Ten per cent discount for Cash allowed off Makers' Price List.

GALVANIZED WIRE NETTING.

CHARLES SMITH,
Saddler and Harness Manufacturer
72, CASTLE STREET, FARNHAM.
Established over 50 Years.

PRICE'S prepared COFFEE
On the French principle.
30 BOROUGH, FARNHAM.

J. A. WARD,
Ready Money Boot and Shoe Establishment,
2, Borough, Farnham.
All Goods Marked in Plain Figures.
2, Borough, Farnham, and at Sutton and Carshalton, Surrey.

FLOWER POTS AND SEED PANS
IN ALL SIZES.
RUSTIC POTTERY,
PROPAGATING GLASSES.
MILK PANS AND DAIRY UTENSILS.

W. C. MILLARD,
CHINA, GLASS, AND LAMP WAREHOUSE,
46, BOROUGH, FARNHAM.

THE LARGEST MANUFACTURERS IN THE WORLD
Colman's Mustard
MANUFACTURERS BY SPECIAL WARRANT TO THE QUEEN
"ASK FOR GENUINE OR DOUBLE SUPERFINE"

WILLIAM PRICE,
WHOLESALE AND FAMILY TEAMAN,
30, BOROUGH, FARNHAM.

PRINTING! PRINTING!! AT LONDON PRICES
GOOD and CHEAP PRINTING
Surrey and Hants News Office, Farnham Surrey.

W. H. VICKRIDGE,
26, HIGH STREET, GUILDFORD.

"GLENROSA,"
A PURE OLD HIGHLAND MALT WHISKY.
Price 42s. per dozen.

HOLDEN'S
BOOT AND SHOE ESTABLISHMENTS.
44, Borough, Farnham.
BOOTS AND SHOES
Your Repairing solicited.

H. LOVELESS,
106, WEST STREET, FARNHAM.
NEW AND SECOND-HAND FURNITURE,
Iron Bedsteads, Carpets, Perambulators, &c.
106, West Street, Farnham.

WILLIAMS'S TAMARIND COUGH SYRUP.
JAMES WILLIAMS,
Pharmaceutical Chemist
Victoria Road, Aldershot

Fire Insurance Society.

Farnham Freehold Building Society.

GEORGE ELLIOTT
WEST STREET, FARNHAM.

DANIEL S. STEVENS.

CHARLES BORELLI,
BOROUGH, FARNHAM.

DAY, SON & HEWITT'S BROWN CHEMICAL EXTRACT

"Bronchiline."

DAY, SON & HEWITT'S RED DRENCH.

"Red Paste Balls."

DAY, SON & HEWITT'S GASEOUS FLUID.

DAY, SON, & HEWITT.

The *Surrey and Hants News* is Surrey's oldest newspaper, founded in 1859 at No. 1 The Borough, Farnham. In the late 1970s the title was bought by Ray Tindle, proprietor of many newspapers nationwide, and converted into a tabloid from a broadsheet. In contrast, the *Weekly Herald*, which was started in 1892, began life as a tiny news-sheet, smaller than a tabloid.

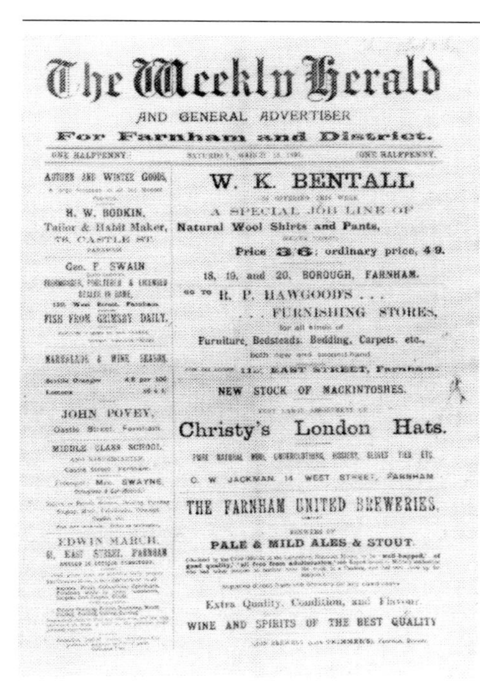

The Weekly Herald

AND GENERAL ADVERTISER

For Farnham and District.

ONE HALFPENNY. | ONE HALFPENNY.

W. K. BENTALL

A SPECIAL JOB LINE OF

Natural Wool Shirts and Pants,

Price 3/6; ordinary price, 4/9.

18, 19, and 20, BOROUGH, FARNHAM.

GO TO R. P. HAWGOOD'S . . .

. . . FURNISHING STORES,

for all kinds of

Furniture, Bedsteads, Bedding, Carpets, etc.,

both new and second-hand

112, EAST STREET, Farnham.

NEW STOCK OF MACKINTOSHES.

Christy's London Hats.

C. W. JACKMAN, 14 WEST STREET, FARNHAM

THE FARNHAM UNITED BREWERIES,

PALE & MILD ALES & STOUT.

Extra Quality, Condition, and Flavour.

WINE AND SPIRITS OF THE BEST QUALITY

H. W. BODKIN,

Tailor & Habit Maker,

78, CASTLE ST.

Geo. F. SWAIN

FISH FROM GRIMSBY DAILY.

JOHN POVEY,

Castle Street, Farnham

MIDDLE CLASS SCHOOL

Castle Street, Farnham

Principal: Mrs. SWAYNE.

EDWIN MARCH,

81, EAST STREET, FARNHAM

The *Weekly Herald*, which celebrated its centenary in 1992, was founded as a tiny newspaper. It covered Farnham and district, and carried eight pages of news and advertisements. In the edition of which this is the front page, M. & J. Tily advertised, as they did in the *Surrey and Hants News* (see p. 51).

A rare programme from the Farnham Repertory Theatre, a forerunner of the Castle Theatre and the Redgrave Theatre. When a group of roving actors arrived in town in 1939 they decided to open up in a building in Castle Street and a number of well known actors and actresses, including Gerald Flood, Philip Latham and Heather Chasen, trod the boards in this tiny, intimate theatre.

The
Bourne and Wrecclesham District
Nursing Association

(In Affiliation with the Queen's Institute of District Nursing and
Surrey County Nursing Association).

•

HOME NURSING SERVICE

Look inside and see what the New Scheme Offers!

Before the days of the National Health Service hundreds of local people paid into private schemes, such as the Home Nursing Service, to help in cases of emergency as well as confinements. The money payable by a weekly wage earner with children of school age was 6s and for other families, including servants, the fee was £1. No infectious cases were covered and a note read: 'The Committee reserve to themselves the right to deal with hard cases and new residents.'

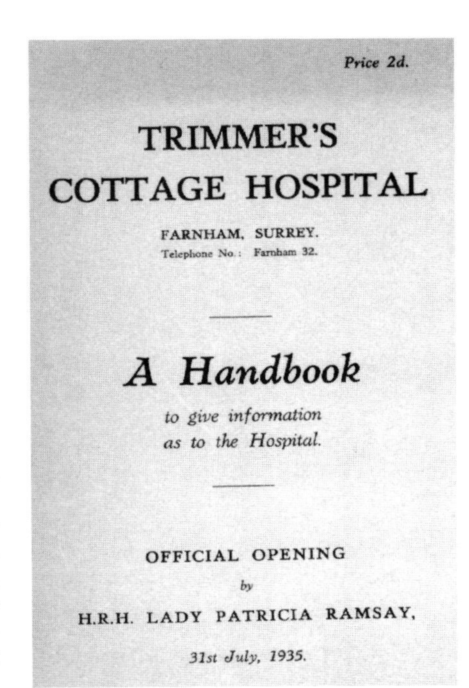

Price 2d.

TRIMMER'S
COTTAGE HOSPITAL

FARNHAM, SURREY.
Telephone No.: Farnham 32.

A Handbook

to give information
as to the Hospital.

OFFICIAL OPENING
by
H.R.H. LADY PATRICIA RAMSAY,

31st July, 1935.

The Phyllis Tuckwell Hospice in Menin Way, now used for the terminally ill, started out as Trimmer's Cottage Hospital, in East Street. The official opening on 31 July 1935 was performed by HRH Lady Patricia Ramsay. This handbook, which cost 2d gave information about the hospital, including its telephone number, Farnham 32. Between 1893 and 1923 six members of the Trimmer family left bequests totalling £23,100 to the hospital.

PROGRAMME

of the

UNVEILING and DEDICATION

of the MEMORIAL

to those from the

PARISH OF HALE

who gave their lives for their Country

in the Great War.

Sunday, August 14th, 1921,

At 6.30 p.m.

On a hot summer evening in August 1921, crowds gathered round a corner of Hale recreation ground for the unveiling and dedication of the memorial to those people from the parish of Hale who gave their lives in the Great War. The band of the Hale and Heath End branch of the British Legion played, and the address was given by the G.O.C.-in-C., Aldershot Command, Lt-Gen the Earl of Cavan. The names of 112 people are inscribed on the base of the memorial, from the First World War, including four Newmans, three Larbys and two Armsworths.

It is more than likely that some of those people whose names were inscribed on Hale War Memorial had worked at William Kingham and Sons Ltd before they went on active service. In this wine and spirit brochure from the firm it is stated that their fine ports and sherries were stored in cellars over 300 years old. There can be few drivers today who realize that crates of vintage wines were once stored only a few feet beneath the pedestrian crossing outside the post office in West Street. Kingham's shop was adjacent to Church Passage.

SECTION FIVE

By the Way

In the past businesses seemed to remain viable for many years. Recently, though, many have lasted only a few months before being forced to close, and once a shop has closed it does not take very long for its memory to fade. It is only in a section such as this, when names and sites such as Cullen's and Timothy White's are recalled, that 'the good old days' return. Not all the firms in this section have gone but those which remain, Elphicks for example, have been much altered over the years.

This row of shops was demolished to make way for Sainsbury's new supermarket and car park in South Street. W.H. Cullen was an old fashioned grocery store where coffee was ground while the customer waited, and where cheese could be tasted before purchase. It was then cut with a wire on a cheese board, to the exact weight a customer required. It was widely believed that a member of the Cullen family married a member of the Sainsbury fold, thus explaining why this shop was lost in favour of the much larger store. The new supermarket was described by a local artist as being designed in the 'Buchenwald Gothic' style, as it was so out of keeping with what it replaced.

This building was demolished to make way for the new part of Swain and Jones' garage on the north side of East Street. On the extreme left a few bricks can be seen of what was once Sturt's wheelwright's shop established in 1810. The rear of West's motor-cycle showroom included part of the old cottage in which George Sturt, the wheelwright, lived.

Downing Street as it was when cars were almost unheard of on Farnham streets. The buildings on the left were mostly private houses; today they are retail premises for pianos, toys, blinds and a beauty salon. The first shop which can be seen on the left is possibly I. Hoptroff, tea dealer, and the shop with a white blind on the front is probably J. Stevenson, draper, outfitter and tailor. Where the youths on the right are watching the cameraman was A.J. Mallam, tailor and breeches maker.

This postcard of Elphick's is captioned, in the corner, 'A Shop in Farnham, Surrey'. It was probably taken just before the First World War. Three lights can be seen on the building, each of which bears the firm's name. These were used so that customers could see the wares even when it was dark.

There was two-way traffic in The Borough when this picture was taken, as can be seen by the cyclist on the left and the horse and cart on the right. The Bush Hotel remains today but the Ship Hotel and public house under the watchful eye of Mr C. Lorkin, has long since gone. The building now houses the Abbey National Building Society. The sign for Frisby's the shoe shop (see p. 58) can just be seen in the background on the left.

A Miss M. Fletcher, of Gravel Hill Cottages, Farnham, received this postcard in September 1924. It shows Knight's Bank (now replaced by a new building for Lloyds Bank). To the right of the bank is the premises used by H. Bodkin, tailor and habit maker, and to the left of it is the building once used as Farnham Girls' Grammar School. On the extreme left is the Bell and Crown public house once run by Mrs M. Collins.

A view up The Borough when Alan Clarke ran a hairdressers at the end of the arcade. The Scotch Wool & Hosiery Stores and Sturt's bookshop were the last shops before the building society at the corner of Castle Street. John Chapman, left, studies the window of Frisby's, the shoe shop he managed for many years. The top hat shows the premises of Hamilton-Jones, and The Borough Bakery sign can be clearly seen.

A rear view of Rose's corn chandlers just as the buildings beside it were being demolished. The shops in The Woolmead can be seen in the background.

A row of shops in East Street, which were among many demolished to make way for The Woolmead complex. Among those shown are Varney's wallpaper shop, the Golden Hind and Farnham Pet Stores, all of which were empty before demolition.

This is the footpath to the central car park which is situated in The Borough, almost facing W.H. Smith. The cottages on the right were demolished to make way for the bedroom extension to the Bush Hotel. The iron steps leading to a first-floor office were the entrance to Farnham Conservative Office until the mid-1980s. In the centre is Frisby's (see p. 58).

Behind the trees is the building once known as The Surrey Knitting Industry works. The houses in the foreground have long since been demolished to make way for Swain and Jones' showroom on the south side of East Street. The occupants of the cottages were probably moved into houses where toilets were indoors, rather than in the backyard as in this picture.

Jack Lewis-Jones, founder of Swain and Jones, on the site which was later to become the company's new workshop. He is standing on the spot where a donkey was buried. It belonged to the sister of Dr Bell of Farnham, who had bought Dogflud Manor (the present Swain and Jones' offices) and had the house converted for her. Miss Bell was a great campaigner for animal rights. During the Second World War this area was given over to allotments.

The demolition of two attractive shops in South Street. They were not very old (as South Street, earlier known as the New Road, was not constructed until 1868), but had great character. They stood almost opposite the Locality Office and adjacent to Gostrey Meadow. Expedier House (see p. 62) can be seen in the background.

The Downing Street Club, at the entrance to the Central Car Park, was demolished in the late 1980s to make way for an office block. Before becoming a club it had been a public house for at least 250 years, first being called The Adam and Eve then The King of Prussia and latterly The Hop Bag. The site is said to be haunted by the ghost of a horseman and carriage.

All the buildings in this picture have been demolished and a block of offices occupies the site. It is at the junction of South Street and Union Road. Morley House is on the left and Expedier House is in the centre.

This view into East Street from The Borough was probably taken in the late 1950s before the north side of East Street was demolished to make way for The Woolmead. A notice on Dewhurst's window states that chickens cost 7s 6d each. Next door is S. Bide and Sons, the florist; the same building was formerly the Ship Hotel (see p. 57). Just as in The Borough, traffic was two-way in East Street at the time this photograph was taken.

The flags in this picture were probably flying for the coronation of King George VI. Timothy White's, the chemist (see p. 69), is in the centre of the parade of shops which also includes two shoe shops adjacent to each other – Holden's and Stead and Simpson. Spencer's, the ladies' outfitter, flies two large Union Jack flags rather than a number of small ones.

There are preservation orders today on any tree which is deemed to be of interest or antiquity, but this has not always been the case. Sir John Verney, a member of the old Farnham Urban District Council, an author and historian, tried to no avail to protect this tree, which once stood on the site at Longbridge now occupied by the police station.

This unusual car, a Nash Metropolitan, registration HF 861, is parked outside the Castle Café in Castle Street in the mid-1960s. The board over the archway shows that this is the entrance to the Castle Theatre. Today the entrance leads to the Pizza Piazza restaurant. The café became a Chinese restaurant which closed in 1992.

Edwin Clarke stands at the door of his fishmongers in Downing Street. To the left of the building runs Ivy Lane, leading to the present Conservative Club – which was formerly a corset factory. Large fowls cost 2s 9d and it is interesting to note that even in a fish shop the assistant, peering through the window, is wearing a stiff, wing-collared shirt and tie.

Stan Phipps, sweeping the pavement outside Nelson and Goodrick's shop in West Street, sometime in the early 1950s. Mr Brown the window cleaner has parked his ladders against the wall of the Farnham Printing Company on the other side of the street. Strip lighting has been installed in the ceiling, but at ground level the shop still looks much as it did before the Second World War.

Speeds the tobacconists, next door to the Queen's Head in The Borough. Every evening, workers returning to their homes at Hale, Heath End or Aldershot, would wait for a bus at this point and, as well as buying cigarettes and tobacco from the shop would also buy the *Evening News* or *Evening Standard* from Cecil, the news vendor from Davies in Castle Street who used to sit on the window ledge here or at the Queen's Head. Speeds is now part of Sevens Wine Bar.

No. 100 East Street, the shop next to the Aldershot and District Traction Company booking office, had already closed when this photograph was taken, prior to The Woolmead development, but the 'Traco' or 'Have a shot and risk it' office remained at No. 101, until it was transferred to the new office in the new precinct. At this time people still asked for Players Please, Tizer the Appetizer, Coca Cola or Rowntrees sweets, but traffic was obviously becoming a problem because there is a 'No Waiting' sign outside the coach and bus office.

There are few pictures of this area to the south of Farnham, with the exception of the Langham Recreation Ground at The Ridgway (or the Ridgeway – modern times and new road signs have increased the confusion about its spelling). It is many years since petrol was dispensed from the Ridgway Road Garage, which also held the Austin/Wolseley franchise.

Thos. Christy and Company, manufacturing chemists, had a large export business in addition to home sales. In this picture, taken in the late 1940s, a large lorry is just about to take dozens of wooden crates, each filled with glyco thymoline, from the factory in Bear Lane to an unknown destination.

South Street before the small shops were demolished to make way for the new branch of Sainsbury – its third site in Farnham. Wilcox, the gents' outfitter (the shop with the blinds extended), moved to East Street to make way for the service road to the new store. The two shops with the unusual roofline belonged to G.E. Day antiques, which relocated to West Street, and Miss Tigwell, who ran an old-fashioned toyshop.

Timothy White's once occupied the site on which the present Boot's the Chemist now stands. In addition to being a dispensing chemist (Cash Chemist, as is boldly written on the left-hand window), Timothy White's was renowned for its hardware, as can be seen by the rows of buckets and tin baths hanging up outside. The right-hand window is crammed with goods of every description. In addition to the services already mentioned, Timothy White's, like its rival Boot's, ran a lending library. The five young ladies, presumably the shop's assistants, posed for this picture with the errand boy who leaned nonchalantly on his delivery bicycle.

The building on the extreme right is the same building which can be seen on page 69, although the ornate ironwork has not yet been added above the shop entrance. Looking down The Borough, towards East Street, can be seen the old Town Hall buildings (centre), a couple of delivery handcarts, one donkey and cart and a bicycle. Newman's the basket-maker is on the left, next to Davis' boot stores. This picture was probably taken before 1888 because Bass beer is being sold in the Queen's Head, which became a Gale's pub in that year.

The Borough in the early 1960s, when buses stopped on both sides of the road. From left to right the buildings were Una's, Burtol Cleaners, the Brown Owl Café, Speeds tobacconists and the Queen's Head.

The sign for Roger's Bakery can just be seen in the background of the old picture of The Borough on page 70. This is the same building as the bakers in this photograph. At one time it had a pickle and jam factory at the back as well as facilities for making boiled sweets, and was a bakery for over 100 years until it was taken over by Kentucky Fried Chicken in the early 1980s. The building is now a dress shop. Next door can be seen Borelli's, the watchmaker and jeweller, who had the Royal Appointment to Queen Victoria.

Moor Park House, where Jonathan Swift, the author of *Gulliver's Travels* and many other classics, was once a secretary to the owner, Sir William Temple. Its owners have included Canon Parsons, who bought it when it was almost in ruins because his late mother, Elizabeth La Trobe Bateman, had lived there for many years before marrying the Hon. Richard Parsons in 1879. Today it is a finishing school for young ladies.

Now a private house in West Street, this was once one of the town's many small, independent shops, which was owned by F.L. Davis and Son. The 'Nelson' name was prominent only because the Davis family sold Nelson Tipped Cigarettes. To the left of this picture, at the spot now occupied by the side entrance to the former St Christopher's School, was a public house known as the Black Dragon.

Maison Radio of Downing Street, to the right of this picture, was a radio and television sales and service firm run by Mr Vincent Trimarco. Shell and BP petrol were sold at the garage, which occupied the site of the present Gateway supermarket. A taxi service was also available from the garage. A two-way traffic system operated in Downing Street when this picture was taken.

The British Drug Houses Ltd commissioned a calendar in 1958 and Annie Martin, one of the town's most famous women, appeared on it in a photograph taken by Kenneth Scowen FIBP, ARPS. Here Annie holds a bunch of daffodils, and if she was true to form she probably thrust them into the customer's hands as she was about to move on, saying: ''ere you are, luv, take these to the old lady wot's ill. They'll make 'er feel better.' The stall was at the bottom of Castle Street. Annie died at the age of 88 years on 4 August 1992.

Firgrove Hill, looking towards the town, when the fir trees were still visible and the only traffic was a single cyclist.

This Raphael Tuck postcard is captioned Heath End Hill, but is better known today as Farnborough Road. The Wellington public house juts out in the background and a small child is sitting on its window ledge. In one of the houses on the left, according to Randall Bingley in his book *Where Dips the Sudden Jay*, lived a lady whose betrothed had been killed in the First World War. She was so saddened by this that she never came out of mourning and used to drop the telegram telling her of the death through her own letter-box at intervals, so that she could pick it up, read it again, and recreate the awful moment continuously until she also died.

SECTION SIX

Real Sports

Much as it might annoy fans of Mike Hawthorn, he is not included in this section headed Real Sports, although there are several pictures of this motor racing driver elsewhere in the volume. Long before the days of the motor car the sports enjoyed in towns and villages throughout the country were of the non-mechanical type: swimming, running, cricket, football and boxing. It is with these in mind that this section has been included. Farnham has sent a number of men and women to the Olympic Games over the years, although none has managed to win a god medal, hard as they tried. One of the best remembered of the women is Barbara Inkpen, who took part in the Games. She was living, at that time, in one of the prefabs mentioned on page 102.

George Hopkins, now a consultant trichologist, was serving in the Royal Navy in 1935. A keen amateur boxer, he is seen here (right) on HMS *Enterprise*, sparring with Dickie Bradshaw, at that time Middleweight Champion of the Midlands. Bradshaw was later defeated by Kid Burke in a contest at Brighton. In 1935 George Hopkins also knocked out the Lightweight Champion of Yorks. and Lancs. in a contest at Madras, India. George, who once sent a letter of advice to Prince Charles to tell him how to avoid going bald, now runs his practice from his home at Little Austins Road, Farnham.

Rowledge cricketers have been renowned, particularly at the Cherry Tree, where there are two teams – one each for Hampshire and Surrey because the county border runs through the public house. There was once a Rowledge cricket team which consisted solely of members of the Parratt family, and sometimes the Parratts played The Rest. This Rowledge team of the 1930s includes Jim Peach, centre of middle row, and Mr Trussler, seated left on the ground.

No names, no pack drill, but this group of cricketers, most of whom are not wearing 'whites', are also believed to have played for Rowledge.

Farnham Swimming Pool soon after it was built to commemorate Queen Victoria's Diamond Jubilee in 1897. It was paid for by public subscription and was designated as a recreational place for the use of everyone in the town.

In the early 1980s the pool was closed down, and those people who wanted to swim had to make do with an indoor pool at the Farnham Sports Centre. The old pool fell into ruin and this picture was taken on the day the demolition contractors moved in. Today there are old people's flats around what was the edge of the pool, but so far the recreational aspect of the pool area, as designated, has still not finally been decided.

Paul Keyworth, who at one time had three shops in Downing Street is holding the microphone in this picture. He now lives in France, but often returns to Farnham. In this picture he is talking to John Ridgway and Chay Blyth, both of whom rowed across the Atlantic. The two rowers are seen here with their wives.

The Farnham White Stars Saturday XI football team in their 1908–9 season, pictured in Farnham Park. Charlie Dean, pictured standing top left, was also well known in Farnham as a plumber. One of his unusual triumphs was finding the solution to a no cold water problem at Farnham Castle. It was caused by a frog which had crept into an open conduit and swum through the main to block the hydrant junction. Charlie worked as a plumber for sixty years.

SECTION SEVEN

War and Peace

From the time when Farnham women were said to have saved the town when it was invaded by Danes and their menfolk were away (at a battle believed to have been at Gong Hill) through to the first two-minute silence in Castle Street during the First World War and the efforts of local people during the Second World War, Farnham has seen itself at war many times within the past 1,000 years. In this section both the famous and the unknown are featured, and the chapter is a tribute to all those men and women who died while fighting for freedom.

Possibly the most famous British face in the Second World War, after Winston Churchill or King George VI, was that of 'Monty' – the Field Marshal. He lived at Isington Mill, just outside Farnham, and upon retirement was frequently seen in the town when he collected his pension from the main post office. His car was usually chauffeur driven and for years had the number plate NAA 1 F. When looked at quickly, this tended to be seen as NAAFI, the initial letters of the Navy, Army and Air Force Institute, a place with branches worldwide at which service personnel could relax, eat, drink and be free from the cares of war for a few hours. In this picture, 'Monty', who was a very short man, can be seen second from the left.

During the First World War many soldiers were based on Frensham Common and around the Great Pond. As in the Second World War, too, many came from Canada (see p. 84). These postcards were made from a photograph by G.E. Langrish, a local man, and were published by R. Sturt and Son, Farnham. Any soldier buying them to send home to his wife or girlfriend would have seen instructions on the back stating that postage was 1/2d inland and 1d abroad.

Millions of components for ammunition packing cases were made at Crosby's in West Street during the Second World War. This operator is using a Belgian machine to cut circles of wood from square blocks.

Basil Crosby (right) set up a Bomb Disposal Unit in Farnham soon after the outbreak of the Second World War. Basil's unit was an offshoot of No. 6 Platoon A Company, Second Surrey Battalion of the Home Guard, which had grown out of the original Land Defence Volunteers (LDV) formed in 1940. This picture shows members of the Bomb Disposal Unit in action. The unit accounted for many bombs, and its achievements were marked by the award of an MBE to Basil Crosby.

Judy de Burgh, her brother, sister and sister-in-law, were all on active service during the Second World War, each in different uniforms. Judy, Anne and Robert were in the WRNS, WAAF and the Army respectively while Edith Moore, who later became Robert's wife, was in the Women's Land Army at Farnham. In the two pictures on this page Judy is above in a photograph taken by her brother-in-law John, a Canadian soldier, in 1944. Anne was photographed in 1940. She married Capt John Praysner of the Royal Canadian Regiment in 1941. The couple had one daughter, Jane, and they emigrated to Canada after the war. John died there in 1970.

Robert de Burgh, who was in the REME, is pictured right, when he was with the British Embassy in Teheran in 1943. Bob was a pupil at Farnham Grammar School and after the war spent most of his life on the technical side of the film industry. His wife is pictured above in her Land Army uniform.

Robert de Burgh, who can be seen on p. 83, was just a small boy when this picture was taken in 1917. His father, also Robert, stands behind the lad who is wearing a woolly hat, probably knitted by his mother, Lucy, who is holding her son. The picture was probably taken in the winter because young Robert is wearing woollen mittens as well as his warm headgear. Robert, senior, was in the Royal Field Artillery, and can be seen on the day he married Lucy Lehmann in the photograph on p. 133.

The little girl in this picture is a niece of the small boy above and grandchild of the boy's parents. The photograph of Capt John Praysner, the Royal Canadian Regiment, and his daughter Jane, was taken in Farnham Park. He was stationed at Bordon when he married Anne de Burgh (see p. 82).

During the First World War these men were in the Civil Defence, and had to practise in their civilian clothes. Although they look old they were only middle-aged, and all came from Farnham and the surrounding villages.

Women worked in the Crosby factory while the men were away fighting, and here they are involved in the manufacture of packing cases for ammunition. The women in their dungarees and turbans were also captured on canvas by John Hutton (see p. 16).

During the Second World War everyone was expected to take part in some form of Civil Defence work as well as their regular occupation. This picture shows the Farnham Post Office unit in 1944 or 1945.

Brigadier-General Campbell lived at Badshot House and for a time was a member of the Farnham Urban District Council (FUDC). When the Land Defence Volunteers (LDV) were formed in the Second World War he joined up at the age of seventy, as a Lieutenant. The unit later became part of the 2nd Surrey Battalion Home Guard. This picture was taken at Runfold when the LDV men were on parade. Mrs Campbell organized a canteen in the Badshot Lea scout hut for the use of soldiers who were billeted in the village.

The Crosby factory's welcome home dinner for those who had been on active service during the Second World War, took place on 9 November 1946. Note the flags of all nations hanging from the ceiling. Only six women can be seen in the picture; two are seated at table, while the other four are, presumably, those who waited on the diners.

Enemy action damaged very few houses in Farnham during the Second World War, which is why this bombed building in Firgrove Hill has become so well known in the town.

REAL

A.R.P. BLACK

Paper **30** inches wide

Only **2d.** per yard

In 2, 3, 4, 6, 8, etc., yard lengths.

TRANSPARENT

"CELLOPHANE" PAPER

For Windows, etc.,

per **3d.** sheet

20 x 30

LANGHAM'S,

114 West Street, Farnham.

Telephone **5265/6.**

Possibly the house above was bombed because the windows were not sufficiently well blacked out to avoid detection by enemy bombers. Although many people bought blackout curtain material to cover their windows others were too poor to do so, and bought paper as in this advertisement. At least one family in Farnham, too hard up to buy either paper or material, had to go without sheets during the war because mother dyed them to hang at the windows. At the end of the war she bleached them and put them back on the beds.

SECTION EIGHT

The Younger Generation

It has often been said that childhood is the happiest and most carefree time of one's life and in most of the following pictures smiles seem to be more numerous than frowns. From the stern, formal school photographs taken in the late Victorian era to the relaxed scene of a class; from the Sunday School tea party in the presence of the vicar to the group outside Sunday School taken a century earlier, these pages recall the younger generation of the past who became the parents, great-grandparents and great-great-grandparents of the children in Farnham today.

Members of the Old Trimmers Day Nursery pictured in 1945 or 1946. In the middle of the top row is Sister Evelyn Mitchell, and next to her in a white apron is Staff Nurse Joyce Cooper. The matron at the time was Miss Curtis, and in the front row on the right is Staff Nurse Merrick who was in charge of the baby section. The nursery was run by Surrey County Council.

The football team from Tilford School who played many games against teams from other villages. Harold Cole is on the extreme right. He grew up to be one of the few non-titled people in Farnham who received invitations to royal events from Queen Mary, Queen Elizabeth (wife of King George VI) and Queen Elizabeth II. The teacher pictured is Bessie Hills, the headmistress. She also attended Harold Cole's 21st birthday celebration.

This A.J.S. motor-cycle combination belonged to the Farnham solicitor, A.J. Stevens. When he first owned it he allowed his children to look at it closely, then on the first day he drove to work on it the motor-cycle was stolen from outside his office. Miriam, John and Michael Stevens, three of his four children, are in this picture.

St Andrew's Sunday School about 1905. In the back row, second from right, is Charles Lehmann and in the centre, partly hidden by the little girl's wide brimmed hat, is Arthur Lehmann.

Young John William Hunt was dressed up, in July 1939, as a nurse for a fête. He was wearing the apron which his mother, Miriam, wore during the First World War when she played at being a nurse. John Hunt, son of Miriam Vesey-Fitzgerald by her first marriage, is now a solicitor. His grandfather was A.J. Stevens.

A group of cheerful youngsters in fancy dress at one of the Christmas parties held by William Kingham and Sons, for the children of their employees. These parties took place from the late 1940s until the end of the 1950s. The baker who won second prize, top row left, was George (better known as Francis) Bowdery.

A class of girls at the former knitting factory in East Street (see p. 60) when the building was used as a school. When the new school was built opposite the Albion, the girls moved along the road a couple of hundred yards into a brand new building with a hall shown in the picture below. Just over ninety years later the school, first known as East Street and later Park School, closed due to falling numbers of pupils, and this was the last Nativity play performed there.

Another group of children in fancy dress at a Kingham's Christmas party (see p. 92), in which Bernadine and Margaret Bowdery, Ann McNair and the Pask twins (the cowboys in the centre) can be seen among other competitors. The lower picture shows some of the same children at the house belonging to the old woman who lived in a shoe, kneeling in the foreground.

Marjorie Beales' class at Park First School, East Street, in 1973 or 1974. Marjorie is pictured far left, near window, and the children are, back row, left to right: Dale Smith, David Royal, Paul Butler, Stephen Cracknell, Gary Wolverson, Timmy Horwill, Steve Cross. Middle row: Stephen Parsons, Stephen Ridgers, Mark Ferguson, Maria Clark, Karina Hayden, Tracy Warren, Lesley Jones, Paul Scott, Nicholas Fry. Front row: Mandy Howard, Lisa Greengrass, Sally-Anne Read, Samantha Doidge, Michelle Cochrane, Sally Cooper, Gillian Alleyn, Hilary Wainwright, Verna Carey, Sarah Culver, Kay Wooderson.

Schola Grammaticalis were the words inscribed on the wall of the building in which these two rooms were photographed. The upper picture shows the sixth form classroom (more reminiscent of a dining room than a place of learning), and the hall is in the lower picture. The building, in West Street, served as the Boys' Grammar School from 1682 when the first headmaster gained a reputation for neglecting his work. He combined the duties of a head with those of a curate at Aldershot. When a new school was built for the boys, the Girls' Grammar School took over the old premises, which is when these pictures were taken. When the girls moved to Menin Way (see p. 46), the building became Farnham School of Art. It is now a centre for adult education.

One of the Christmas parties held in Hale Institute for the children of members of Hale Young Wives. This celebration was probably in 1969, when the Revd Michael Sellors (second from right, standing) was the incumbent in the village. Extreme right is Lily Goacher, whose husband later became the police superintendent at Farnham. Betty Watts, the group's leader, is on the vicar's right, while Jean Parratt is to the right of Betty Watts.

The 'queen' in this group of children at St Andrew's Junior School, West Street, now Potter's Gate School, is Wendy Parratt, daughter of the 'young wife' above. Every year, under their teacher Mr E. Paye, the pupils at St Andrew's School put on a superb production at Christmas which they performed to parents.

The boys pictured above, on one of the three-feet long photographs which were the vogue at grammar schools at that time, entered a wide variety of occupations and professions – after completing the statutory term of National Service, which had to be undertaken by almost everyone in this section of a 1950 picture. Fourth from the left in the back row is Guy Bellamy, who became an author and journalist. In the fifth row from the back, eighth from left, is Ted Parratt, also an author and journalist. Ted and Guy worked in concert as editors of the *Surrey and Hants News* series of newspapers for several years, after Guy had been the only editor for a considerable time. Needing more time to write his novels he finally left the newspaper in July 1991, leaving Ted in sole charge. Others in this group include Robin Broach, a metallurgist; Michael Comben, garage owner; Wil Harland, bank official; Ian Bolt, tomato farmer; Tony Bolt, Rushmoor councillor; John Cherriman, barrister; George Hone, nurseryman and public house owner; and David Lea OBE, deputy General Secretary of the TUC. The headmaster at the time this picture was taken was Mr F.A. Morgan (see p. 134). For a comparatively small country town grammar school Farnham has had an enviable record of Old Boys who have achieved distinction in many spheres, including Surgeon-General O.E.P. Lloyd, the school's only VC; Jeffrey Tate CBE, international conductor and a qualified doctor; Dr C.F. Garbett, Bishop of Winchester and later Archbishop of York; Charles Borelli, noted townsman and Harold Falkner, architect, both of whom strove to enhance Farnham's Georgian image, and Sir Eric Rideal MBE, Professor of physical chemistry at Kings College London. These are only a few who took as their motto *Nisi Dominus Frustra*. Farnham Grammar School was founded before 1585 and continued until it became a sixth form college in the mid-1970s.

Admiral Lord Nelson's phrase, 'England expects every man to do his duty', was often heard in the past, and these children from Wrecclesham looked very nautical and ready to answer their country's call if it came. The event probably took place on Empire Day soon after the First World War ended.

Jugs from washbasins in bedrooms were brought into operation at the table when this picture of children from Stoke Hills was taken at a party in Farnham Park. Judging by the bunting it was probably for a coronation or royal jubilee.

Roman Way estate was started soon after the Second World War ended, and for a while work stopped when the Roman villa and bath were found. This picture was taken at the time of the coronation party in 1953. When materials ran out for brick-built houses a number of prefabricated homes (known as prefabs) were constructed on land to the rear of this picture. The green on which the children are sitting was used every November as the site for an estate bonfire on Guy Fawkes' night, 5 November, until Waverley Council prohibited public bonfires of this type around 1985.

SECTION NINE

Our Best Friends

It has often been said that the dog is man's best friend, but other animals are equally faithful, cats for example. However, it does not matter which animal one gives one's heart to; there is a special bond between man and animal which cannot be priced or explained. In the following pages some of the animals which have been seen on the streets of Farnham are given pride of place.

The circus came to town forty years ago and the sight of ten baby elephants walking in procession from Farnham station to the circus ground in Farnham Park drew crowds out into the streets. Even if one could not afford to go to Billy Smart's Circus the parade of animals was available at no cost, and they can be seen in this picture as they passed the entrance to Gostrey Meadow in South Street.

Throughout the war and well into the 1950s meat was rationed. This picture was taken at the Farnham Cattle Market in South Street in 1954, on the day that fatstock was on sale to butchers for the first time since meat rationing was introduced in 1940. For many years all slaughtering had been done by the Ministry of Food, with the butcher as a retailer. Mr A.V. Lee, on the left in a trilby hat, conducted the sale.

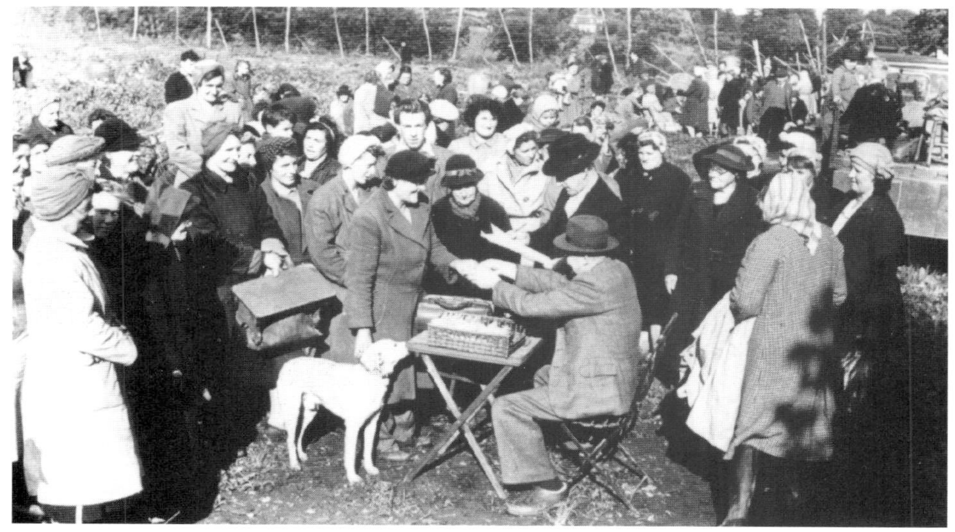

The dog looks on expectantly while his mistress, Mrs Varney from Folly Hill, is paid out after hop picking in the Beavers Hop Ground (site of the present West Surrey College of Art and Design). Mr H.C. Bide is handing her the hard-earned cash. Hops had been particularly difficult to gather in September 1950 because many of the bines had been flattened by storms two weeks before this picture was taken.

Tommy Sawkins, pictured here with two Badshot Greys, was a competition ploughman and one of Alan Tice's best carters. Alan, pictured below when he was a boy, built up a stable of Greys which he entered in local horse shows and ploughing matches. This picture was taken at Badshot Lea.

Alan Tice, from Badshot Lea, used to ride his pony, Joey, to Farnham Grammar School every day in 1916. The pony refused to make the journey along by Snailslynch and Darvill's Lane to reach the school, so Alan had to ride him through the town. Alan wore a bag on his back in which was corn for Joey as well as his previous night's homework. The pony was stabled in an old shed at the school during the day, although it frequently escaped and could be seen munching the grass on the school cricket pitch.

A Stevens family picture taken in Guildford in 1923. Father, better known to Farnham's business fraternity as A.J. Stevens, has his arm around his daughter Miriam's shoulders. His wife, Mary Catherine, has her arm around the youngest son, Michael (see p. 42), while son John looks as if he is ready for a game of cricket and Lancelot the eldest son is on the right. Everyone is named except the family's best friend, the dog in the foreground.

THE FARNHAM DAIRY LTD.

Guaranteed MILK and EGGS from Producer direct to Consumer.

PRODUCTION.

OUR OWN
TUBERCULIN TESTED HERDS AT WISHANGER, CHURT

Are Always Open to Inspection

→

DISTRIBUTION.

NEW LAID NATIONAL MARK EGGS

FROM OUR OWN POULTRY FARM.

Guaranteed to reach our Customers within 48 Hours of being Laid

The advertisement above, concerning cows and chickens, speaks for itself.

SECTION TEN

Revolutionary Forces

From the time that John Henry Knight built his petrol driven motor car at the Reliance Works in West Street, one of the first vehicles of its type in the country, Farnham's streets have never again been clear of cars. In 1992 the most frequent complaint from residents is the lack of parking space in the town. It has not always been the motor car, though, that has transported people through the streets: horses and carts, buses, lorries, motor-cycles and sidecars, and even a hovercraft on a transporter have all been seen. The traffic problem is not a phenomenon of the 1990s, though: see the frontispiece drawn in the 1930s, sixty years earlier.

Edward Giles, at the wheel of this car, was known as The Bacon King of Farnham because he had a number of shops in the area. In the back seat of the car is his wife, and next to her is Basil Norman Giles who bought the garage opposite, known as Calloways, in 1925. At that time it had a fleet of taxis but many horseshoes and wheels still remained there, from when a landau service operated from the site. This picture was taken in the front of Clovelley, Shortheath Road, and Cecil Giles is on the motor-cycle.

A head-on collision at one of the town's most dangerous turnings – the junction of Weydon Lane with Wrecclesham Road, close to the railway bridge. The onlookers, apart from the man with his bicycle, probably nipped out from Abbott's, the car manufactory, whose works is in the building on the right.

The long-awaited Farnham bypass opened in the early 1960s and crowds stood on the bridge at Firgrove Hill to watch the vehicles pass under it. This junction is very narrow and forces the four lanes of traffic at Hickley's Corner to filter into one, going westwards, within a few hundred yards of the Hickley's junction. The bicyle parked on the left belongs to the man who took the photograph.

An early 'Have a shot and risk it' bus, which ran from Aldershot, through Farnham and on to Haslemere. The photographer was from Bramshott. Military personnel are in the vehicle and outside it, so it is possible that some soldiers from Aldershot were out for a trip to the countryside during a leave period in the First World War.

A. Robins & Sons Ltd, a firm which still operates in Farnham from an office near Farnham railway station, took a contract to move some particularly long items, as can be seen here. This picture is believed to have been taken close to the office, which could be the building in the background.

This car and attractive young lady driver formed part of the Christmas display at Swain and Jones in East Street, in 1923.

Swain and Jones opened in Farnham in 1908, on the south side of East Street. An attendant is at the sole petrol pump and is about to fill up the tank on the very uncomfortable looking car with solid disc wheels.

John Henry Knight, one of Farnham's most inventive sons, had one of the first petrol-driven cars in Britain constructed at the Reliance Works, West Street, in 1895. In 1985 the car, now housed in the Motor Museum at Beaulieu, was returned to the town for the special Year of Transport exhibition held at Farnham Museum. This picture, however, was taken by John Henry Knight himself, at his home in Runfold, almost a century ago.

A service van used by Swain and Jones in East Street, when they specialized in Austin cars.

An early motor-cycle and wicker sidecar, which was seen frequently on the roads of Farnham in the 1920s.

William Kingham and Sons' lorries in the warehouse at The Hart, about thirty years ago. When the firm closed down this warehouse was demolished to make way for the Safeway car park.

Jo Simmonds, Farnham's first professional female photographer, took over the Eugene Fuller Delaunay Studio in West Street during the First World War, after Eugene was blinded in action. She took this picture outside her home in Firgrove Hill. Four soldiers, one sailor and a civilian male all seem intent upon a quick roadside repair to one of the three motor-cycles being used, about 1918.

A chauffeur at Hollowdene, Frensham, in a picture which was taken by Mr Sturt of Millbridge.

One of the Yellow Bus Service vehicles which plied its way around villages in the 1950s. This vehicle was approaching Farnham via Cutmill, but probably the most used service for this company was that which travelled from Farnham Station to Guildford, via Seale and Sands.

An entry for the Farnham Carnival when even the wheels of the carriage were decorated with flowers. The picture was probably taken in the early 1930s and the form of four horse-power travel was followed by a larger beast in the form of a lorry.

Calloway's Garage at Shortheath when three different petrol brands were on sale and the shop/office was in the shed to the left of the picture.

An early passenger vehicle on its return journey from Hindhead to Farnham.

In August 1959 the first hovercraft passed through Farnham on its way to the Farnborough Air Show. It was transported on a flat bed trailer owned by Bakers of Southampton, and shop assistants left their counters to pop out and see this novelty pass by.

Thomas Browning's van may not be photographed well, but this is, nevertheless, an interesting picture of a vehicle which was the pride and joy of its owner. Mr Browning operated the Steam Bakery from Abbey Street, the thoroughfare which all southward bound traffic from Farnham had to traverse, before the building of the New (South) Street in 1868.

SECTION ELEVEN

Village Life

Although Farnham is now a town it can claim to have the oldest village so far discovered in Britain within its boundaries: five mesolithic pit dwellings were found here in the 1930s. The residents of Rowledge (once known as Rough Ditch), Wrecclesham (where the vagabonds hid in the forest), Hale (where squatters lived on the common), Heath End, Badshot Lea, The Bourne and Weybourne are all villages around the mother centre, and each has a different type of community spirit.

The girls of Badshot Lea Sunday School, photographed while enjoying a treat in Farnham Park in 1910. Although Farnham Park is less than two miles from the children's home village it seemed like a different world when they were in the charge of their Sunday School teachers, Alice Pullinger, Mrs Allen and the two Misses Green, each of whom wore their best hats for the special occasion.

Lily Guppy, pictured with her uncle, Tom Guppy, at Badshot Lea in 1911 or 1912. They are pictured in the grounds of a cottage on the site of what later became Beech Tree Drive.

A mother pushes a pram (far right of picture) followed by a toddler, in the middle of the road at Rowledge, sometime in the 1920s, when traffic was light compared with the present day. The Farnham Coaches coach, parked in The Square, outside the Hare and Hounds public house, which was owned by Farnham United Breweries, was among the first of the regular services from Farnham town centre to Rowledge. This route was later taken over by Aldershot and District Traction Company's buses.

The lady in the trap is Mrs N. Turner, wife of George Turner who was once licensee of the Cricketers at Lower Bourne. Although the trellis at the back has been replaced several times since this picture was taken in 1890, some still remains today on this building now owned by Jeff Lee and George Hone (see p. 98).

The opening of Hale Tennis Courts, to the rear of the Institute, which was built about a century ago can be seen here. The lady in the centre, wearing her widow's bonnet may be the same lady as in the picture on page 131; some of the men look familiar, too. Although these residents of the village appear to be wealthy there was a lot of poverty in Hale too, particularly in the tiny cottages at Hoghatch and closer to Heath End in the terrace which was known as The Huts. About 400 yards from the scene in this picture is Bethel Baptist church in Bethel Lane. Here, 150 years ago, the pastor would walk from Kingston to Farnham every Sunday to preach from the top of a dung hill until the chapel was built. He would then walk back to Kingston in the afternoon. Details of the names of those people who lived in Hale and who died in the First World War can be found in the booklet featured on page 54. The memorial on which their names are engraved is only a few yards from where this photograph was taken but the dark shadow of a world war had not reached Hale at this time.

Wrecclesham Pottery, which has changed little since it was founded by Absolom Harris in 1873. It is still a thriving business and is now in the hands of the fifth generation of the Harris family. Pots are still made by hand, the height determined by a twig sticking from a piece of clay stuck to the wall beside the potter's wheel.

As cars speed down Sandrock Hill today it seems almost impossible to think that eighty years ago, where the gap can be seen in the wall on the left, draymen would stop their wagons here and let horses pull barrels of beer along the river, transporting the beer to the Bat and Ball public house in the valley. It was scarcely accessible then to anything other than pedestrians.

The lace curtains, high collars for both the men and the women, and the waxed moustache make this picture of Farnham author George Sturt (right), with his parents and sisters, a typical example of Edwardian photography.

Hollowdene, Frensham, in a postcard view taken by Sturt of Frensham, was one of the many big houses in the area. So many servants were needed to keep it in good order before the days of electric light, electric cleaners and washing machines, that a retinue of servants 'lived in', sleeping in the attic rooms, so that there was always someone on hand to answer the room bells when they were pulled.

Most of Frensham was once supplied with milk by the Newmans, who ran Kennel Farm Dairy. Milk was ladled from the big churn into the smaller containers depending on how much was required by each householder. Once transferred to the half-pint, pint, quart or gallon buckets it was then tipped into the householder's own receptacle.

Shortheath, at the junction of Shortheath Road, Echo Barn Lane, Sandrock Hill Road and School Hill. The small tree which can be seen protected on the left is the same tree which was planted in the picture on page 144.

The Mort family of Frensham, taken at the end of the First World War. Back row, left to right are: George, Enid, Eric and Margaret; seated, Ida Mort and the Revd Ernest Mort; and at the front Basil Mort. The five children of Ernest Mort and his wife had all been born at the vicarage in Frensham. George was ordained and became a missionary, dying in Africa in 1940. Eric was a teacher and did much to pioneer education work in Nigeria, although when he returned to England he spent much of his time painting and helping with the Scout movement. He died in 1969. Basil was an accountant who died in 1979. Margaret and Enid were the best-known Morts, both of them devoted members of St James's church, Rowledge. Enid was a nurse and a member of the Women's Institute, and Margaret worked at Frensham Hospital in the Second World War.

The new Trimmers Hospital, which opened in Menin Way, Farnham, in 1935, was aided by funds raised at a carnival. Here, members of Rowledge Women's Institute pose for a picture with their banner and one of the carnival's marshals (right). A few typically local names are evident among these ladies, including Mrs Glashier, Mrs Jarman, Miss Morgan, Mrs Farr, Miss Mason, Mrs Bicknell, Mrs Thompson, Mrs Fry, Mrs Wolstenholme, Mrs Ridgeley and Mrs Knight.

A view along The Street, Wrecclesham, when there was not a vehicle in sight. On the right is the Royal Oak, once run by 'The King of Wrecclesham' Jonathan Parratt, so called because of the correct way in which he dressed for formal occasions. The public house, at the time this picture was taken, was owned by Farnham United Breweries.

This pub at Wrecclesham, The Bear and Ragged Staff, has a sign on the side showing where most of the Courage ales came from sixty years ago – Alton.

This cheerful group of regulars from the Hop Bag public house in Downing Street (see p. 62) travelled by one of Gudge's coaches, from The Bourne, when they went on a day trip to Portsmouth. The driver was Tom Wilmore but he seems to have temporarily given his white-topped cap to a young lady fifth from left. The coach behind, from White's of Camberley, has liquid refreshment on the roof in the form of three crates of Watney's Pale Ale in flagon bottles.

Cricket on Tilford Green became a humorous affair when, in a celebrities versus the village match in the early 1970s, Anita Harris's dog decided that the stumps was a better place than a tree to relieve himself against. Kent Walton (see p. 146), the famous wrestling commentator, is on the right, wearing a pullover, and between Anita and one of the players is Ann Flood, wife of Gerald Flood, the actor. He played, among many other television and theatre roles, the part of Inspector Mahmoud in *The Ratcatchers*. The Barley Mow is in the background. This green and the public house were also used in the television production of *England Their England* and the village's famous oak (see p. 130) was featured in a booklet devoted to information about the one pound coin, which was issued by the Royal Mint. Although Gerald Flood died in 1989 his widow still lives in Farnham. His son, Simon, also lives in the town although his other son Tim, who followed his father into the theatre, but on the administration side, is now at a theatre in the north of England.

Men, women and children spent hours in the hop gardens picking the green/gold cones that were (and still are) used to flavour beer. At one time Farnham hops were the most expensive in the world, because of their subtle flavour and light colour, which tied in with the vogue for so-called 'light ales'. When the season was poor, though, the workers knew that however hard they picked they would not be able to make enough money to buy a pair of shoes for each of their children for the winter. Sometimes there was discontent and, occasionally, a strike. Between 1910 and 1920 there were several bad years for hops and a strike at one of the gardens in Lower Bourne eventually resulted in the pickers being given an additional farthing per bushel, a miserly sum for the work involved. Nevertheless it was sufficient to convince the pickers that they should go back to work.

Summerhill Cottage, Frensham, typical of the many small cottages which were set in their own neat gardens, in fields throughout the Farnham area a century ago.

It seems hard to believe that a small butchery shop at Shortfield, such as this owned by Mr Heath, could warrant having such a large stock of meat. However, the big houses in the area, with the retinue of servants which was needed, accounted for the major part of this butcher's business.

This photograph was taken in the early 1920s and shows the famous Tilford oak, which is believed to have been written about in the Domesday Book. The oldest inhabitant of the village, when the picture was taken, is sitting on the seat under the tree.

Frensham Camp: countless numbers of tents occupied by the military at Frensham during the First World War. The coarse heathland and sandy soil must have been very hard for exercising and pitching tents, particularly in view of the heavy uniforms and boots worn by soldiers at that time, but extra business was brought to the area, particularly at local pubs in the evenings, so the soldiers were welcomed.

This somewhat stiff and starchy group is sitting on the terrace at the side of Hale Institute for a special occasion. Undoubtedly the Caesar family, who were very influential in the village, are represented in the picture, which must have been taken in high summer judging by the boaters worn by a number of the men. The picture was probably taken at about the turn of the century.

My husband's cousin, Frank 'Punch' Parratt, who appears in my first volume about Farnham, took this picture of his fiancée, Kathleen Wilkinson, at a high point at Burnt Hill, The Bourne, in 1928. Frank, who died in 1988, commented that looking at this picture revealed that housing was quite scattered at the time, and that the pine forest, which now covers the area, was then in its infancy. Kath and 'Punch' were married in 1933.

Frensham Mill, almost a century ago. The wagons are loaded with sacks, each bearing the name of the mill.

The man with the high position in life is Mr F.C. Smith who, with Mr T. Willis, is pictured erecting the string framework for the coming season of hops. This scene was common in and around Farnham in springtime. The long bundle contains pre-cut lengths of coir yarn, which would be tied to the upper wires by the man on stilts, while the man on the ground would tie them to the lower wires. This was known as the Butcher method and is being used here in one of A.P. Tice's hop gardens in the Guildford Road, Farnham, in 1953.

SECTION TWELVE

Salmagundi

It is unlikely that any other book has ever had a chapter headed with the word salmagundi, yet there have been thousands which used a synonym for it – miscellany. I have chosen the more unusual noun because the section has such a diverse selection of pictures, ranging from the most famous spiv of all, Arthur English, through to selling bricks to help build a theatre, and a tailor sitting cross-legged, sewing a suit. There is always a group of pictures in a book of this type, which do not fall into any particular category, so in this specific case salmagundi will cover them.

Lucy and Robert de Burgh leave Farnham parish church after their wedding in 1915. He was an architect on war service in the Royal Field Artillery; she was an assistant at Spencer's, the ladies' outfitter, which was situated at the junction of Downing Street and The Borough. Before joining the army, Robert was trained as an architect by the famous Harold Falkner. Lucy's parents were Lewis and Ada Lehmann of Farnham.

Albert Aslett photographed in his typical tailor's pose, eyes down, needles and threads pinned in his lapel, and an inch tape measure round his neck. He was a military tailor from Long Garden Walk, and was believed to have trained under H. Bodkin, who had a tailor's in Castle Street. Married to Aimee Lehmann, he was probably the last tailor in Farnham to sit cross-legged on a table to work in the full view of passers-by.

This man, known affectionately by generations of youngsters at Farnham Grammar School as 'Skull', was the headmaster, Mr F.A. Morgan. In *A History of Farnham Grammar School in Surrey*, one former pupil, J.M. Aylwin, described Mr Morgan as being 'fanatically fit', and 'a brilliant teacher and born leader'. A pair of gates are now at the entrance to the Farnham Sixth Form College (formerly the Farnham Grammar School) and are known as The Morgan Memorial Gateway.

Clearly a formal occasion of some sort for Farnham Fire Brigade, in the 1930s. Those identified are, from left to right, Edward (Ted) Brooker, -?-, Harry H. Greentree, Mr Elderfield (captain of the brigade), -?-, -?-, G. Goolding, C. Friend (in beret), T. Spencer, N. Goolding. The men are in Castle Street, outside the Coach and Horses and are being watched by, among others, a youth, extreme left, wearing a Farnham Grammar School cap. His headmaster would probably have frowned at a pupil in uniform with his hand in his trouser pocket.

During the Second World War, when Crosby's in West Street was playing a large part in supplying packaging for munitions as well as temporary buildings and other equipment, there was a need for additional accommodation in Farnham for all the extra workers which the firm needed. Therefore tents were pitched on part of the Memorial Hall ground and they can be seen in the foreground of this picture.

The ironmongers in Castle Street, Robert Dyas, was formerly known as Tily and Brown. This is a picture of Mr Tily taken by a photographer named Olive Edis, who apparently had branches in Sheringham and Cromer in Norfolk as well as in Farnham. Mr Roy Armstrong from Shortfield, Frensham, is proud that his mother worked for Mr Tily as a housemaid until she married in August 1919.

Mr George Elphick (1843–1921), founder of the West Street firm, Elphicks, as he was when he came to Farnham from London, in 1881. The current family member, Allan Elphick, is the fourth generation to sell household textiles, clothing for women and children, toys and perfume from No. 13 West Street.

Five years separate the wedding photographs on this page and on page 139. The posed group with the pine tree backdrop are, back row, left to right: Herbert Mansey, Mrs Mansey, Norman Goolding, Cliff Lucas, -?-, Reg Goolding, Mrs H. Goolding, Howard Goolding, -?-, Mrs Elkins, Fred Goolding, Daisy Paris. Middle row: Frank Goolding, ? Shepherd, ? Lucas snr, Mrs Lucas, Francis John Goolding, Fanny Goolding, Leasen Goolding, Mrs Paris snr, -?-. Front row: Eva Goolding, Rhoda Carter, Gordon Goolding, Phil Lucas, Winifred Lucas, Gertrude Goolding, Miss Lucas, Mrs Leasen Goolding, Miss Head. Seated: Roger Lucas, Les Gains, -?-, Miss Head, Cody Goolding, William Bertal. This picture was taken in 1923.

Kathleen Slaughter, with her grandad, Lewis Lehmann, after the wedding of her aunt, Lucy Lehmann, to Robert de Burgh, in 1915. Lewis was a watchmaker and silversmith with the famous Charles Borelli, who held the Royal Appointment to Queen Victoria.

The 1953 coronation was a special time in local schools and in almost every one pupils had photographs taken in front of a commemorative backdrop. In this picture, taken at Badshot Lea School, Barbara Bryant (who married and became Mrs Wright), aged fourteen years, poses with a pen. Barbara lived in St Mary's Place, East Street, as a child. Her daughter, Judith, became a traffic warden in the town.

The young Alfred Julius Stevens, known to everyone as A.J., when he was on holiday at Cowes in the Isle of Wight. Mr Stevens first practised as a solicitor in South Street, moving later to No. 5 Castle Street where the firm of Stevens and Bolton still operates today.

This wedding group, posing on the steps of Church House, was snapped on a wet day in 1928. Back row, left to right: Cody Goolding, Mrs Budd, Francis Goolding, Mr Budd, Fanny Goolding. Front row: Miss Head, Norman and Kitty Goolding, Gertrude Goolding, Miss Head, Miss Budd.

In 1948 four men sat down to discuss the formation of a new club in Farnham: they were Messrs R. Cox, F. Sherman, F. Ritsert and F. Willie. The club, known as Farnham Old Timers, began and Frank Willie was the treasurer. Mr Willie died in 1975. His widow, Florrie, then continued as a committee member until her death. No old-time dance, whether at Owen Hall, the Memorial Hall or the Central Club hall would have been complete without Frank and Florrie Willie dancing gracefully around the room.

More than 150 members of the Boys' Bridge paraded to the Farnham Methodist church to pay tribute to the company's founder, Sir William Smith, on the 97th anniversary of his birth. They can be seen passing the Albion Hotel, East Street, having marched from Hale. Dolley's Nurseries (now Dollis Drive) is on the right.

Roman Way residents gathered in the rain on a Sunday morning to listen to Alec Brade. The reason for this unusual gathering was because Farnham Urban District Council had decided to introduce a differential rents scheme to its tenants and many protested. In spite of the problem outlined here at least twenty homes on the estate are still occupied by the original residents in 1992, forty-five years after the houses were built.

Around 200 people gathered outside Church House in Union Road, to hear the declaration of the poll for the General Election when Mr Godfrey Nicholson, Conservative, was successful in the Farnham Division. When Mr A.A. Minns, the deputy returning officer, announced Mr Nicholson's majority of 10,198, the crowd sang 'For he's a jolly good fellow'.

Farnham Urban District Council bought the Happy Home, a public house at Lower Bourne, for demolition, so that there could be an improvement scheme at the site. The Happy Home formerly stood opposite the Fox, which is still trading and is on the left of this picture.

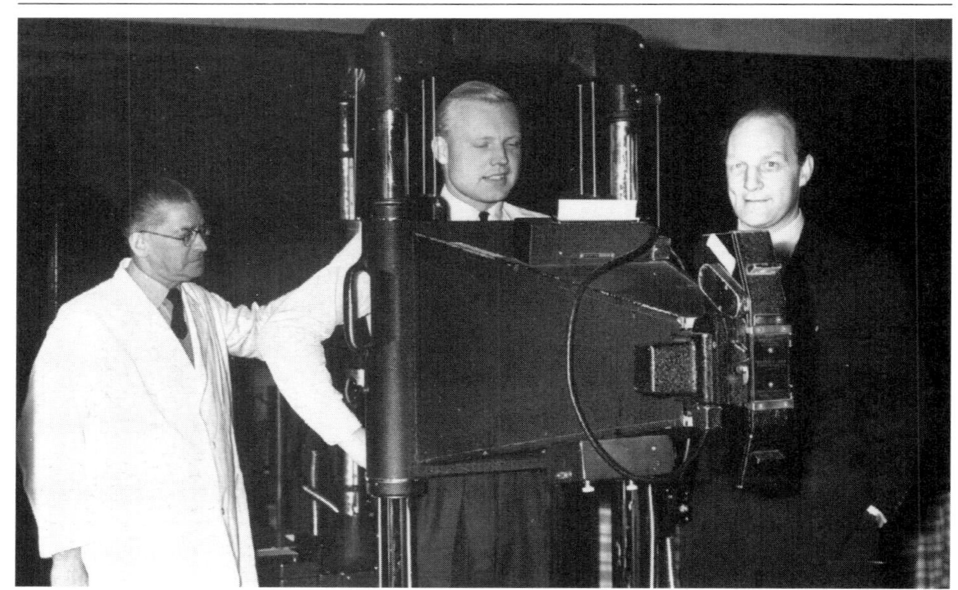

In the mid-1950s mass radiography took place, with mobile units going to many towns on a regular basis to take x-rays of the chests of both men and women. Many people, though, were still scared of such devices so racing driver Mike Hawthorn, the town's best known sportsman, showed he had no fear of it and was first in the queue in June 1956. Here he can be seen with the radiography superintendent Mr A. Goss, left, and Mr R. Clark, right.

Green's Dental Laboratory was founded by C.J. Green, a young dental mechanic who ran the business from his home before he moved into a building on the Farnham Trading Estate. This picture was taken in the laboratory which backed on to Hurlands Close.

Mike Hawthorn appears to be making a citizen's arrest in this picture taken with Arthur English, the comedian from Aldershot who received the Freedom of his home town about forty-five years after this picture was taken. Arthur was known as a spiv and wore very large 'kipper' ties which were made by his wife and reached down to his thighs. The trophies are some which Mike had won in motor racing (see p. 146).

The lady on the steps of Farnham Castle is Vicky Noakes, wife of John Noakes of TV's *Blue Peter*, who, as Vicky Binney, modelled on the steps of Farnham Castle in the early 1960s to promote the firm of Catherine Fenez in Castle Street. Vicky, her sister Sarah and mother Margaret still own the ladies' dress shop today.

When King Edward VII was crowned, in 1902, an oak tree was planted at the junction of four roads, School Hill, Shortheath Road, Sandrock Hill and Echo Barn Lane, close to a point now occupied by the Shortheath bus terminus and waiting room. Pictured are Mr Fry (holding the tree) and Mrs Lucy Clark, who each received a telegram from the King, marking the occasion. The Revd Keeble, Vicar of Wrecclesham is pictured, with arms folded, above Mr Fry. Though the oak tree shown above was felled by Aldershot and District Traction Company, who built the terminus, there was such a public outcry that another was planted, which is still growing today.

The bread delivery man with his horse and cart looks as if he is at the end of his day's work. There is no bread in his basket and he looks tired. The Farnham and District Industrial Co-operative Society operated from Nos 11 and 12 Castle Street in those days, until it was taken over by Davies the newsagent, under which guise it continued for decades.

Downing Street looking into Lower Church Lane. A coal merchant's cart is outside the building which is now a chemist, and the sign for the Feathers public house can be seen to the right of the lamp standard. The date of the picture is unknown but it was probably taken about the turn of the century.

This picture of Mike Hawthorn was taken four years before he won the World Motor Racing Drivers' Championship in 1958. Here Mike is seated at the wheel of The Snozzle, a Cooper-Bristol in which he won two races at Goodwood on Easter Monday in 1952. In the twelve-lap Richmond Trophy race he came second to Gonzales of Argentina.

Kent Walton, known to millions as the commentator for professional wrestling matches on television, knocked over a pile of pennies in The Lamb, Abbey Street, sometime in the late 1960s. In the background the man whose head is to the right of Kent's head is Ray Fulford, a local barber.

SECTION THIRTEEN

Team Spirits

Much can be achieved by a man or woman who operates alone, but even greater are the works carried out by a group, whether it is through nursing, teaching or collecting money for charity. In the following pages there are teams of many types, from those helping to plant a tree on behalf of the WVS to a group of Old Girls who have returned to their old school in the hope of recapturing the team spirit which they valued so much in their youth. From the severity of the school teacher of the Victorian era to the informality of a group of contestants for a personality prize, the feeling of unity and togetherness is brought over in these pages.

A line-up of St John Ambulance volunteers at a special presentation ceremony. In the group are Win Ariss, Beatrice Sawkins, Sister ffoulkes, Vi Collins, Joyce Searle, Mrs Bates, and Joan White, a cadet. The names of the other ladies are not known.

A reunion at Farnham Girls' Grammar School, probably in 1951. The group includes teachers and former pupils, with the headmistress, Miss Dorothea Inman, standing on the extreme left. She is wearing a light-coloured coat. It is interesting to note that the majority of the women are wearing hats and either wearing, or carrying, gloves, even though it was late spring. Miss Inman was the school's head for 17 years, from 1947 to 1964 – longer than any other head in the school's history.

Although the majority of entrants in the Lions Club Miss Farnham competition in 1971 opted for evening dresses, two young ladies dared to wear the fashion of the day – miniskirts.

A line-up of staff at Hale School, then known as Bishop Sumner School, taken around 1880. The headmaster, Mr Eli Caesar, is third from left in the back row. The very young female teacher on the extreme right seems to be wearing clogs, and both she and her neighbour are wearing slightly shorter dresses than the older females.

The Red Cross on parade in West Street in the 1950s. The Cosy Café can be seen in the background. The women in the foreground are just approaching The Hart and are being watched by Ted Hyde and his wife. Ted formerly worked for the Wey Valley Water Company. He died in 1991.

Part of the funeral procession of Supt Simmonds, a former Farnham police officer. The front of the Singer car has wreaths on it and the funeral took place at St Thomas-on-the-Bourne church. Supt Simmonds and his family lived halfway up Firgrove Hill.

For a time in the late 1960s and early 1970s the Farnham Town Show was a feature of midsummer in the town. This view of the floats winding their way up Castle Street to the park was taken in 1970. At that time the Coach and Horses, on the left, was a Courage pub. A Farnham Division St John ambulance can be seen, third vehicle from right.

In 1972 the Castle Theatre company was playing *The Queen's Highland Servant*, by William Douglas Home. During the play's run, from 18 April to 6 May, the cast took time off to publicize the selling of bricks to help raise money for the new Redgrave Theatre. The group in this picture, which was taken on the recently demolished Rose's site, shows Doreen Andrew who played Queen Victoria (on horseback). Chris Reeks, centre, proffers a brick to the cameraman. The man on the extreme right is William Whymper.

Ringing in the New Year in Farnham parish church early in the 1950s.

Farnham Girls' Choir on the occasion of its 21st birthday. The founder and conductor, Mary Joynes, is on the right at the front.

A notice on the side of this St John Ambulance picture reads: 'This ambulance was on duty in London yesterday for the coronation of Her Majesty Queen Elizabeth'. Mr Herbert Mansey, a sergeant in the brigade, is next to the ambulance. The picture was taken in 1953.

Catherine Duvall, known to her friends as 'Puck', can be seen with a spade as she planted a tree, on behalf of the WVS, at Farnham Hospital. In March 1959 she had tea at Buckingham Palace with 499 other WVS personnel for the 21st birthday of the association. She was awarded the MBE for her wartime service in the WRNS and for over thirty years was a member of the Bourne British Legion, becoming chairman and later president of the Women's Section. She now lives in the house, a former shop, shown on page 72.

The occasion that this picture marks is not known, but it shows, through the trees, Owen Hall, which was situated above Farnham Co-operative in Union Road. It was clearly a celebratory occasion because the flag is flying on the parish church and there is bunting around the meadow. However respectful the crowd of adults seems to be, though, the two small boys in the centre of the picture seem to be playing around: one is lying on the grass of Gostrey Meadow. Judging by the fashions in clothing, the picture was probably taken in the 1930s, perhaps either for the coronation of George VI or the Silver Jubilee of George V coming to the throne, which took place in 1935.

Farnham Horticultural Society held an outing around 1930. This picture was taken at Bide's in Runfold before the men went off for a day without their wives.

Today Farnham is twinned with Andernach in Germany, but in the early 1950s its twin town was Haren in Holland. A stone commemorating this twinning is in the Farnham–Haren garden in South Street. This photograph, taken in Castle Street, shows the Farnham– Haren committee and Dutch guests about to embark on a coach trip.

This is the cast of *Trial by Jury* which was performed by the Farnham Operatic Society in 1948. The judge was played by John Daykin, the plaintiff was Eileen Daykin and the defendant was Leslie Halliday. Others in the cast were James Kimber, Peggy Dymott (who later played the piano for dances at the Owen Hall in Union Road), Valerie Dabek, Pat Austin, Evelyn Williams, Joan Patrick, Irene Skuse, Eileen Barnard, Edward Lacy, John Evans, John Harding, F. Northover, F. Harman and the Revd Cream.

This line-up of young ladies would scarcely pass muster in the 1990s but in 1935, when Mrs Vernon Cheshire produced a revue at the Bourne Hall, the girls were considered to be highly desirable in their polka dot dresses and ballet shoes. The lady in black is the producer.

Farnham has had many itinerant workers, especially in the hop gardens. They were despised by some local people, so it would seem to be the least likely place to find a gypsy orchestra. In 1938, however, a group organized by Reg Tracy, centre, on cello, was known as The Gypsy Orchestra. They played at many local fêtes and summer functions. Edward Griffith, a local freelance photographer, who was also a musician, can be seen playing the accordion with the group, though he was also part of a trio called The Marshall Brothers Plus Jean.

Caryl Griffith, an actress and dancer, who once aspired to be a journalist, is seen here in a photograph taken by her father, Edward, behind one of the model trains which he held so dear. The picture was taken in the mid-1950s. Caryl is a granddaughter of the Revd Thomas and Constance Griffith (see p. 159).

Before the days of television and radio a game of bagatelle would have been considered an ideal way in which to spend an afternoon or an evening. In this picture, taken inside the Bourne Vicarage in 1930, the Revd Thomas Francis Griffith, Vicar of St Thomas-on-the-Bourne, watches his wife, Constance, as she tries her hand at the board. On the right is Beatrice Griffith.

The four people who conclude this volume have all appeared in it earlier as children. In 1985 Lancelot Stevens, left, was 77, John was 72 and Michael (the tiny boy in a tunic on page 42), was 70. Miriam, to whom this book is dedicated, was 74, sitting happily with her brothers for this picture, taken in Farnham by Martin Rice. Miriam, a friend who provided many of the pictures, died before this book was completed so it seems appropriate to end it with her picture.

Acknowledgements

This book has been made possible by the co-operation of friends and relatives who have willingly put their treasured photographs at my disposal. Although this is my third picture book about Farnham it has still not been possible to use every print I have been loaned. I should like to thank the following people for giving me permission to use their pictures and for helping with information for this volume:

Alan Dadley • Marie Siggery • Roy Armstrong • Chris Hill • Clem Keddie
Peggy Chapman • Mrs Cornwall • Judy Dye • Maurice Elphick • Jean Hogg
David Colston • Judith Briggs • Wally Aspden • Irene Cole • Dorothy Gilliam
Win Ariss • Miriam Vesey-Fitzgerald • Joyce Stephenson • Honor Duvall
Jonathan Durham • Edward Griffith • Wendy Hobart • Warwick Swales
Percival Pelling • Arthur Brown • Dennis Stone of Farnham Castle Newspapers
Myrtle Birch • Ann Flood • Mary Joynes • Chris Shepheard • Keith Dolley
Stella Bolt • Jim Tice • Angus Campbell • Tom Little • Ted Hyde
Frank Ambler • R. Giles • Mesdames Stonehouse, Jefferies, Smith and Newell,
Museum of Farnham • Mrs Ena Watts • Jane Chia • Margaret Mullery
Bernadine Collins • Annie Martin • Nora Blissett • Sheila Phillips
Peter Lewis-Jones • the Goodridge family • Doug Tanner
Mr and Mrs R.H. Foster • Edward Griffith
Martin Rice and Downing Street Studios • Don Rimmer • Nellie Stephens
Ted Parratt, my husband.

I should also like to acknowledge the works of other authors who have written about Farnham in the past and on whose knowledge I have based some of my text. These include Bill Ewbank Smith for *Victorian and Edwardian Farnham*, George Sturt for *A Small Boy in the Sixties*, John Henry Knight for *Reminiscences of a Country Town*, *Life Let Us Cherish* by Mavis Batey, *Where Dips The Sudden Jay* by Randall Bingley and *Farnham Buildings and People* by Nigel Temple. If anyone has been left out of these credits I apologize, and will acknowledge them in the future.